RETAKING
EDEN

PASTOR D

WESTBOW
PRESS®
A DIVISION OF THOMAS NELSON
& ZONDERVAN

WestBow Press books may be ordered through booksellers or by contacting:

WestBow Press
A Division of Thomas Nelson & Zondervan
1663 Liberty Drive
Bloomington, IN 47403
www.westbowpress.com
844-714-3454

ISBN: 978-1-6642-1214-5 (sc)
ISBN: 978-1-6642-1215-2 (hc)
ISBN: 978-1-6642-1213-8 (e)

Library of Congress Control Number: 2020922263

Print information available on the last page.

WestBow Press rev. date: 11/13/2020

Foreword

In the beginning God created the heavens and the earth.
The earth was formless and void, and darkness was over
the surface of the deep, and the Spirit of God was moving
over the surface of the waters. Then God said, "Let there
be light"; and there was light. ...God saw all that He
had made, and behold, it was very good. And there was
evening and there was morning, the sixth day.

—Genesis 1:1–3, 31 NASB

Pastor D (and Pastor M) are not the missionary mentors you always
wanted. They are the designated disciple-makers you never knew you
needed. If your search to find the heart of God for your life and mission
in Christ has led you to this moment where you have cracked open this
book to glance inside, then I want you to know that Jesus must have a *big*
plan for your ministry. Because, although this author is a dear friend and
tenured associate of mine, my joy in recommending this read for your
edification runs much deeper than that fact.

It has been my observation that most people are initially attracted to,
and feel impacted by, missional thinking for a couple of typically similar
reasons. Maybe your youth group went on a missions trip to Mexico or
India, and you came back home on fire for God, determined to give the
rest of your life to serving humanity and spreading the gospel. Maybe a
missionary couple from the Polynesian islands or West Africa visited your
church; and as you stared at those pictures of desperately impoverished
children and heard the stories of how the gospel has never been preached
in those villages, your heart burned within you. Maybe you immediately
collapsed in tearful surrender at the altar that night, crying, "Here I am,

Lord; send me." Maybe you journaled your impressions for a couple of years as you sponsored a family in a feeding program.

But eventually, you could no longer ignore the growing call to do something more about it personally. Whatever your story of how you came to be reading this book, you need to know one thing. You are pondering enlisting in the most elite squadron within the most highly trained Special Ops division of the army of the Lord. From the day you take your first concrete step into answering the call, your life will never be the same. And it will never belong to you again. The tears, fears, financial struggles, relationship strains, rejection, discouragement, depression, anxiety, and an ever-growing sense of your own insufficiency to accomplish the task for which you have been sent are all sure to be greater than you could ever anticipate or imagine, by an order of magnitude. Negative? Nah. I'm not being negative. I'm telling you something you need to know about why God has mercifully placed this book in your hands. Because the joys, triumphs, testimonies, windfalls, and breathtaking and heartwarming experiences will also so far exceed your dreams, that you will finish your life without one hint of regret for having given it away.

If that is so, then why should I tell you these hard truths about the arduous journey upon which you have embarked, if it will indeed lead to such a heavenly outcome? Because you need to know that the toll of the mental, emotional, spiritual, and physical roller coaster of life in your mission field can only be sustained by a soul that is grounded in a truth big enough, a cause so grand, that it far outweighs these light and momentary trials with an eternal weight of glory. I have never been a foreign missionary. But I *have* been a church planter in one of the most spiritually dark fields on the planet.

I am also honored to be a close friend to several missionaries. I have walked with them through the dark valleys of self-doubt, discouragement, even despair, malaria, witchcraft, hopelessness, bribery, corruption, grief, marital stress, and soul-crushing loneliness that have attended their way. And I can tell you that in your darkest hour, your feet will have to be planted on a foundation built to withstand these pressures, pressures that cause the vast majority of missionary candidates to quit before they have truly begun. So … this raises the question. What foundation is firm enough to stand?

As the boy-king David pointed out when all the armed forces of Israel cowered in fear before the champion of Gath, the answer lies in knowing and understanding your cause. The cause you represent must be so much bigger than the giants you will face that every threat of opposition seems to you as nothing in comparison. There is ultimately, only one Cause in the universe so grand, so meaningful, and so worthy that every other consideration dissolves into stark irrelevancy before it. And the only way to understand that cause is to grasp a rather obvious but deeply underappreciated theme of scripture—the grand theme, in fact.

The first few sentences of the book of Genesis, quoted in my opening above, cover a vast and indeterminable span of time; and they set the drama of the Bible squarely in context as one part in a series, in a vast cosmic struggle that predates our own world as we know it by untold eons. God created everything. Something happened. Everything was destroyed. Darkness reigned. Nevertheless, God remained present. Then God spoke into the darkness. Light came into the world. *"And it was evening, and it was morning, the first day."* You see, God has been waging a cosmic war against His enemies for ages. And every time God creates goodness, evil comes along and seeks to frustrate the light and order with darkness and chaos. Night falls. Then, painted upon this canvas of death, God begins yet another masterpiece of life.

While it's human to think the beginning of a thing is when the sun rises on it, when light comes to it, God places evening before morning in the days of His working. God always begins where darkness has fallen and pierces the night with hope and grace. Someday soon, His light will prevail in an ultimate victory, vanquishing darkness and chaos forever. His kingdom will be reestablished without end, and heaven will come down to rest upon a renewed creation for an eternity without interruption. Eden will bloom again: Paradise found.

This is the one cause that is big enough to quell every fear, silence all doubt, override all depression, and outlast any weariness. This is God's cause—the redemption of all created things from the curse of sin and death and their restoration to unity and fellowship with the Creator. This purpose alone represents the heart of God. This plan alone reveals the heartbeat of His divine desire. This cause alone contains the divine spark that can bring dead things back to life, revive dreams, restore hope, and preserve faith within the heart of a warrior who has been wounded on the battlefield of mission. This is the endgame. This is God's "why": recapturing Eden.

Soon the King will make war on the blight of sin which has wreaked havoc through selfishness, dishonesty, lust, and greed upon the garden of His love. Soon He will destroy the destroyer, and Eden will bloom again.

> After these things I heard something like a loud voice of a great multitude in heaven, saying, "Hallelujah! Salvation and glory and power belong to our God; because his judgments are true and righteous; for He has judged the great harlot who was corrupting the earth with her immorality, and He has avenged the blood of his bond-servants on her."

> And a voice came from the throne, saying, "Give praise to our God, all you His bond-servants, you who fear Him, the small and the great." Then I heard something like the voice of a great multitude and like the sound of many waters and like the sound of mighty peals of thunder, saying, "Hallelujah! For the Lord our God, the Almighty, reigns. Let us rejoice and be glad and give the glory to Him, for the marriage of the Lamb has come and His bride has made herself ready." It was given to her to clothe herself in fine linen, bright and clean; for the fine linen is the righteous acts of the saints. Then he *said to me, "Write, 'Blessed are those who are invited to the marriage supper of the Lamb.'" And he *said to me, "These are true words of God."

> And I saw heaven opened, and behold, a white horse, and He who sat on it is called Faithful and True, and in righteousness He judges and wages war. His eyes are a flame of fire, and on His head are many diadems; and He has a name written on Him which no one knows except

Himself. He is clothed with a robe dipped in blood, and His name is called The Word of God. And the armies which are in heaven, clothed in fine linen, white and clean, were following Him on white horses. From His mouth comes a sharp sword, so that with it He may strike down the nations, and He will rule them with a rod of iron; and He treads the wine press of the fierce wrath of God, the Almighty. And on His robe and on His thigh He has a name written, "KING OF KINGS, AND Lord OF LORDS."

And I saw the beast and the kings of the earth and their armies assembled to make war against Him who sat on the horse and against His army. And the beast was seized, and with him the false prophet who performed the signs in his presence, by which he deceived those who had received the mark of the beast and those who worshiped his image; these two were thrown alive into the lake of fire which burns with brimstone. And the rest were killed with the sword which came from the mouth of Him who sat on the horse, and all the birds were filled with their flesh.

---Revelation 19: 1-2, 5-9, 11-16, 19-21 NASB

Soon, He will set up His kingdom as the garden of the universe, producing an eternal harvest of life, peace, love, and joy. Soon we will be in His Eden restored.

Then I saw a new heaven and a new earth; for the first heaven and the first earth passed away, and there is no longer any sea. And I saw the holy city, new Jerusalem, coming down out of heaven from God, made ready as a bride adorned for her husband. And I heard a loud voice from the throne, saying, "Behold, the tabernacle of God is among men, and He will dwell among them, and they shall be His people, and God Himself will be among them, and He will wipe away every tear from their eyes; and there will no longer be any death; there will no longer be any mourning, or crying, or pain; the first things have passed away." And He who sits on the throne said, "Behold, I am making all things new." And He *said, "Write, for these words are faithful and true." Then He said to me, "It is done. I am the Alpha and the Omega, the beginning and the end. I will give to the one who thirsts from the spring of the water of life without cost. He who overcomes will inherit these things, and I will be his God and he will be My son.

Then one of the seven angels who had the seven bowls full of the seven last plagues came and spoke with me, saying, "Come here, I will show you the bride, the wife of the Lamb." And he carried me away in the Spirit to a great and high mountain, and showed me the holy city, Jerusalem, coming down out of heaven from God, having the glory of God. Her brilliance was like a very costly stone, as a stone of crystal-clear jasper.

---Revelation 21: 1-7, 9-11 NASB

In the meantime, Eden is within us. The kingdom reigns wherever two or more of us are gathered in His name. *That* is the true heart of missions, the cause that overcomes the world.

Remember the former things long past, For I am God, and there is no other; I am God, and there is no one like Me, Declaring the end from the beginning, And from ancient times things which have not been done, Saying, "My purpose will be established, And I will accomplish all My good pleasure"; Calling a bird of prey from the east, The man of My purpose from a far country. Truly I have spoken; truly I will bring it to pass. I have planned it, surely I will do it.

---Isaiah 46: 9-11

You hold in your hands the diary of a hardened warrior. Written in the grand tradition of the letters of Paul to Timothy and Titus, this book represents the passing of the torch on a relay race back to the future of God's plan from the beginning. Generations of missionaries have been forced to learn the lessons contained in these pages the hard way, by trial and error, through painful experience, in the school of hard knocks. That includes the author. I know. I was there. The degree is worth the world. But the tuition is unnecessarily high.

If you will let it, this book will become a primary expression of the fatherhood of God in your life. You will come back to its dog-eared pages a thousand times in the next ten years. Each time, your understanding will be refreshed by your growing experience. Someday, many years from now, you will finally realize how much pain and heartache you have been spared by this writing, as you journey through His world on the mission to carry Eden to the ends of the earth.

Unlike the generations before you, you are not alone in this journey. The Lord is with you. That we know. But through this book, He has sent you the voice of a father. Read it carefully. Understand it prayerfully. Apply it diligently. As it was in the beginning, so shall it be in the end. And when your ministry in this life is accomplished, in the end you will find yourself back at the beginning, at rest in the Arms that have carried you as they have Pastor D and Pastor M. Paradise found. Welcome to Eden. "Well done, good and faithful servant. Enter into the joy of your master."

—Pastor Shules Hersch, Lead Pastor, Promiseland Church

Preface

Retaking Eden is not my plan; rather, since the fall, it is and has always been God's plan to restore our relationship with Him. Sending Jesus to Earth so that we may be clean and have eternal life with Him was not an afterthought. God's endgame is to fully restore us and bring the kingdom of heaven to Earth. Our job is simply to prepare the bride of Christ for His return. Eden is not simply a place to run naked, eat fruit, and nap under trees. It is where we have a perfect relationship with God Himself. Retaking Eden is our ultimate goal and the one thing worth sacrificing our lives for.

To understand the intent of the letters written to Macy and Mark reproduced in this book, it is more important to know the *why* of Macy and Mark rather than the *who* of Macy and Mark. The why is more a matter of legacy. Although my desire is to continue to lead and disciple the next generation, I am coming to realize that to the multitudes of youth, life may seem a gallimaufry, an evanescent conundrum of disjointed events seemingly leading to an eternal demise. Even those who sought my tutelage passed only briefly on their way to somewhere else.

I myself was left wanting as we read scores of droll, irresolute missionary biographies during our time of preparation. The formula became stale and unfulfilling as the monotonous story lines unfolded: Under protest and against all odds, the missionaries strode boldly into the mission field, eventually their wives succumbed to illness, and they barely escaped death as they led thousands to Christ before they themselves died. My heart begged to know how they felt during their failures and successes, as well as how they processed such loss and tragedy while they continued on with their missions.

My hope and faith is to lead as many as possible to the knowledge of the enthetic nature of the Holy Spirit as it relates to one's calling, to provide both direction and inspiration toward that end, and to share our process and adventures in God's kingdom. The greatest deterrent to fulfilling our lives' mission is our complicit agreement with the lies the enemy spews into our minds concerning our worth and merit as we serve our Lord Jesus Christ and His lost and hurting children.

When all is said and done, the only things that will have mattered are how well we followed the Greatest Commandment and walked out the Great Commission. This is the message I would want my children, grandchildren, and great-grandchildren to understand. It is my message to Macy and Mark and to all those who have the heart to follow Jesus Christ.

All events depicted here are real; however, the characters' names have been changed.

My Dearest Macy and Mark,

I was so happy to hear the news that you have undertaken the greatest adventure, which is to fulfill God's purpose for your lives. A Masters Commission is a wonderful avenue to learn and grow in the knowledge of Christ. I am somewhat concerned that your education there may lack the balance necessary to transition smoothly into a foreign mission's post. Because of this concern and many others, I entered into fervent prayer on your behalf. I am agreeing to your request for mentorship through written discipleship training, and I am convicted that sharing our experiences in hope and faith will help you seamlessly transition into missionary life in the third world.

Lesson 1: Why

So You Want to Be a Missionary

It has been said that Haiti is the most difficult mission field in the world. Quite frankly, I was skeptical of this claim, considering the horrific conditions in the slums of Southern India, the demonic presence in Northern India, the omnipresent danger in the Middle East, the drug and sex trafficking in the former Soviet Union and Southeast Asia, and let us not forget all of sub-Saharan Africa with the child soldiers, diseases, and widespread starvation. How could this little island nation be more difficult than all those places? Half of all missionaries in Haiti leave within their first six months; 80 percent within the first year. Sadly, only 5 percent make it past five years.

With the exception of the child soldiers, Haiti has all the problems found in those other regions and more. Most obvious is the relentless physical toll exacted on one's body here. A myriad of pathogens maintain a continuous assault through air, ground, water, and food. Outside the major cities, adequate supplies of clean water, quality protein, and variety in vegetables is a struggle. The heat and humidity are oppressive, draining energy reserves and preventing restful sleep.

The emotional toll is no less damaging as countless problems arise daily. The need is so great it is overwhelming at times. We were taught that we should allow others to participate in our ministries and that we were denying people the blessings that come through giving. However, very few people ever respond to the needs we present. You cannot adequately explain the conditions there. Most people would never believe that living situations could be this bad.

For me the tragedies are the most difficult to endure, usually followed by months of vivid nightmares. Burying children gets old very fast; likewise the constant cries for food from the malnourished children. Murder, rape, and sexual and physical abuse are all too common in our community.

We have created a safe place here at Project Eden for the hundred-plus children we look after. Yet it never seems like enough. Currently, we are in the process of repairing the swings and building a shower for the kids so they do not have to bathe in clear view of the public highway. A dozen or so children are in need of books for school and have been sent home and/ or beaten, even though we paid their tuition in full.

The spiritual assaults are by far the worst, daily trying to push us to the breaking point. Whatever it takes to stop your ministry will be thrown at you, including death, which is just as effective as having you quit. There are nine primary spirits that came from Africa during the slave trade, and they are painfully apparent. Anger, sexual perversion, alcoholism, suicide, and fear are the five that are the most obvious in the native population; combined, they create an extreme oppression that permeates the atmosphere. Pleading the blood of Christ and His love is by far the most effective weapon against this oppression.

We recognize all these attacks—physical, emotional, and spiritual— but the most difficult attack to overcome is loneliness. The culture is so foreign that no matter how much love we pour into the children, it can never replace those we love at home. I believe Haiti is the most difficult mission field on Earth simply because it is the loneliest place on Earth.

Why stay? you may ask. The answer is simple. If you are, were, or will be a parent, would you leave your child if you were suffering physically, emotionally, or spiritually? Of course you would not! God called us, sent us, and gave us several hundred children who think of us as second parents. The fight is so hard because the reward is so great! If this were easy, I would be worried that we missed God's will. The truth is that we are right in the thick of it, in the trenches, fighting hand to hand, as we were always meant to. This country belongs to Satan, and if necessary God will take it back the same way Iwo Jima was taken, one foxhole at a time!

I wrote this during our second year of full-time service in Haiti, when we were in the thick of the battle. It begs the most important question for you both—why? Your why must be divine purpose. And you not only must be fully cognizant of the why, but be fully committed to the why as well. Please pray, and when you can earnestly respond with your why, we will continue your training.

In His love,

Pastor D

My Dearest Macy and Mark,

I pray this letter finds you both well. I liked your answers to my question. To reduce pain and suffering and bring the lost to the knowledge of Christ is a great answer, although I felt it a little too cookie-cutter for ones such as yourselves. There is a bigger picture, one in which we retake Eden. I am alluding not to a physical capture of the actual ground but rather to a spiritual victory. When Satan tempted Eve in Genesis 3:6, she desired with her eyes, she longed to be wise (powerful), and she brought Adam into sin with her. It is easy to blame Eve, but she was created from Adam, who was her head. He had the ability to say no, but instead he became complicit in sin with her. We all know the price we paid—and the ultimate price that Jesus paid for that moment. God's plan has always been to redeem us and restore the perfect relationship that we once had with Him. Our ultimate responsibility as the bride of Christ is to prepare for the Bridegroom's return.

Everything hinges on our mission to retake Eden. This is not anyone's sole responsibility; however, we all play our parts. As we reduce pain and suffering and bring the lost to the knowledge of Christ, we must hold this bigger picture in our minds. In the heat of the battle, remembering our ultimate purpose gives us strength and the ability to overcome temporary losses. Focusing on the big picture is what sustains a missionary. We were not always missionaries. Let us return to the moment God first moved in our hearts.

About a decade ago, I was praying in the pews at our church. I told God I was not afraid anymore and asked Him to please use me. I may digress at a later time into why I was previously afraid. For now, I will forewarn you that if you pray a prayer from your heart that lines up with the Word of God, He will surely answer your prayer. Around this time, God gave me a scripture to stand on, Ephesians 2:10: "We are God's workmanship [masterpiece], created in Christ Jesus for good works, which God prepared beforehand that we should walk in them."

Soon everything began to change both in church and at school. We began serving in whatever capacity we could, eventually becoming active in thirteen different ministries. I began a club for my students to actively serve the community and the needs of the less fortunate among us. About a year and a half later, I met a family from California who had recently joined our church. The father was a pastor and ran an active mission in Haiti. He asked me to join him to evaluate the school on the mission property. The following accounts are of both my and Pastor M's first visits to Haiti and our induction into missionary work.

Lesson 2: Answer the Call

Faith and the Unknown

The apprehension of the uncertain mingled with the uneasiness of flight slowly gives way to excitement as the mountainous landscape of Haiti begins to unfold on the horizon. As the plane makes its final descent, additional features of the terrain come into view. The land seems lush and tropical, with the ocean similar to every Caribbean island that we have ever visited, except where the rivers empty brown, polluted, parasite-infested waters. The diffused pollution appears to engulf the coast and inundate the shoreline.

Soon we touch down smoothly and taxi to the nearby airport terminal, which is running at only about 50 percent because of the recent earthquake. Immigration and customs both occupy a large room with no air-conditioning or clear lines. The mass of people just pushes forward like a herd until eventually reaching an agent.

Once out of the terminal, the compound manager gives me the biggest hug I have ever received from a male greeting us. I am a little uncomfortable at this but quickly accept that this is the genuine love from God pouring out through him. As we turn into the streets, it is immediately apparent that we are in a third world country. The first UN tank rolls past, followed by a Hummer with an M60 mounted on top. We see many more military vehicles as we wind our way through the broken streets. Filth and litter are everywhere, in places knee deep. Port-au-Prince (PaP) is a city constructed for four hundred thousand inhabitants, which now holds more than six million residents. A comment is made that the city appears cleaner than ever before; I smile quietly to myself.

A rat scampers toward the buildings as we round a corner. I see one man punching another through an open car window. My anxiety is climbing as we reach the large market and surrounding tent city. There are hundreds if not thousands of small vendors selling food and sundries. Apparently, food is not in short supply. Rather, it is the rampant unemployment that drives Haiti's deplorable poverty. Sometimes when we snap pictures of the locals, they want to be paid for taking their picture, feeling as though we will profit from it. The tent cities are scattered everywhere, along with the surrounding shantytowns. I comment that the shanty looks like better housing; the reply is that I'll change my mind once the rains begin. There is no public sanitation, and as a result an extreme amount of human feces will wash into the water supply during the rainy season, inevitably causing a massive cholera outbreak. We see people bathing in the murky parasite-riddled river alongside hogs and other animals. Downstream, I notice children filling water containers from the same nasty river. Most disease in Haiti is waterborne, although malaria is a pervasive threat as well.

Soon, we have left the hustle and bustle of the city behind and are moving rather quickly through the beautiful countryside. We are welcomed lovingly when we arrive at the Children's Home. I immediately notice that the oppressive feel of the city has lifted and soon realize that the protective hand of God is over the property. The main house was obviously designed and built by Americans. With the exception of the entryway, the rest of the house is smartly tiled. I find my bed to be comfortable, and two fans are at my disposal.

This evening concludes a three-day revival at the compound church. We eat dinner with the founders and their children, both of whom are employed on the premises as the compound manager and school superintendent. I am impressed with them and feel that they are solid choices to manage the compound affairs. We are served spaghetti with meat sauce that is quite good, even by Italian standards. One of my greatest concerns was the quality and quantity of food I would be served while in Haiti. My other main concern was safety; however, while we are doing God's work, we are covered by the provisions stated within Psalm 91. There is no fear here in the Children's Home—only the love of Christ.

Prayer and music practice precede the service by almost two hours. We arrive right on time, and my presence is requested on stage as an honored guest. I am very self-conscious and uncomfortable with this request. In response to my discomfort, I am told I may sit where I like. I weigh the selfishness of my actions against my need to be comfortable, choosing the American way; I consider my own needs first and find a place among the congregation.

We are very closely packed, and it is hot and uncomfortable on the wooden benches, but then service begins, and everything but God's presence melts away. It's striking how completely the congregation is in accord with the praise and worship. Everyone is on cue, and the rhythm and praise envelop me. The service lasts for more than two hours, and I am exhausted as the women's choir begins their rehearsal for morning worship.

The crazy rooster begins his crowing at around three in the morning, making for a short night. I am very tired, but once the shower has been liberated from a giant spider, the frigid water snaps me awake. Breakfast is light, consisting of toast and incredibly delicious cherry juice along with the best coffee I have ever tasted. Service begins at eight, and everyone is in their Sunday best. The girls all look as if they have dressed for Easter. Today is the fourth anniversary of the compound church's inception. Service is almost five hours long, but I enjoy every moment, except for the numbness in my backside.

A little girl stares blankly at me. She is not sure what to think of the Q-tip sitting in the congregation. She reaches a finger toward my hand. As I raise a finger to meet hers, she pulls away. A minute later her finger reappears, and this time I remain still. She touches my hand to see if the *blan* (white) feels the same as she does. Soon we are engaged in a round of peekaboo over the pew. Later, a sharply dressed young girl, perhaps twelve, sits next to me. She is obviously hot as she is continuously fanning herself. I grab my battery-operated fan and point it toward her, engendering a coy smile that lights up her face as she shyly whispers, *"Mesi"* ("thank you"). As the temperature keeps rising, so do the energy and presence of the Holy Spirit. Person after person rises from his or her seat to offer either a testimony of praise or a song to the Lord. The Lord quickens me to something that had eluded me thus far; there are almost no old people in the service.

Later, as we walk up the hill toward the main house, I learn that a woman from the church has passed away and that another recently died giving birth to her fourth child while being severely malnourished herself. As we continue to walk, two preschool-aged girls hold our hands; we pause momentarily, so I may view one little girl's facial scars, left by the Guinea worm infestation, which mar her otherwise beautiful little countenance. I decide then and there that along with my wife, Pastor M, I will bring only small groups of youth here, allowing significant relationship-building time to offset the third world trauma they will witness. Small groups will be much easier to manage; besides, constant supervision and discipleship are of the utmost importance in this environment.

After lunch, we walk to part of the compound located across Route #2, which is the main southern highway. We find numerous children in ragged clothes; however, a young boy named Ronny grabs my attention. He has Down syndrome, and we are concerned that if food becomes scarce, he will not be fed. Haitians feed their families quite differently than Americans. The father eats first, since he must be able to work. This is followed by the mother and the children, from oldest to youngest. Survival is the family's priority, so more capable providers move higher on the food chain.

We finish the afternoon by taking some of the children to the beach at Locul, the south's version of a shantytown, located on an otherwise beautiful beach. We have time to discuss the challenges facing the school while sharing our visions for it. I am slightly distracted by the smell of feces; the reason soon becomes apparent as I watch a young child squat on the beach to defecate. With no public sanitation within the shantytown, the beach serves as a giant toilet.

As my last morning here begins, I find myself already becoming reflective. The multitude and magnitude of the problems in this place are overwhelming and must be dealt with one at a time. My last official act is a visit to the school, which unfolds much as I expected. The children are very well behaved, and the teachers are acting in a professional manner. I am a little unnerved as I walk behind the open-air classrooms; a little girl turns her head almost completely around with the evilest look I have ever seen in a child. This reminds me of a scene from *The Exorcist*; however, although slightly shaken, I continue my observation.

Once school ends, the children have time to laugh and play as lunch from the feeding kitchen is distributed. We say our final goodbyes and head back to Port-au-Prince for our final evening. The American-built compound has ten-foot walls topped with razor wire and a heavy steel gate flanked by two armed security guards to protect against the evil and violence outside the walls; yet, I can't help feeling less secure here than I did at the Children's Home. As the plane ascends, my emotional and physical exhaustion climaxes while my brain ponders how quickly I can my return.

Birthing the Heart of a Missionary

Loaded with supplies and gifts, we begin our journey. I am prayerfully expectant that Pastor M will fall in love with Haiti as I have. We are greeted with open arms at the airport and wind our way through the streets of Port-au-Prince, I ask Pastor M what she thinks, and she responds that it is not as bad as she had imagined. My heart sinks as I realize that I described what I had seen in such detail that she was fully prepared for what she was witnessing.

I'm very happy to see that one of the compound children is with us. Her English is better than my Creole, but not good enough to engage in conversation. I open my iPod to help bridge the barrier gap. She begins to play with it, and within five minutes, she seems to have mastered it. She rests her head on my shoulder as she scrolls through my playlist. She tires quickly, curls up on the bench seat with her head on my leg, and dozes off. As the truck maneuvers around the many road hazards, I find myself tightening my grip on her, much as I would do with my own children. I glance down at her as my thoughts drift to what type of future she will have. Will God use this bright, loving child for His glory, or will she succumb to the horrors of disease or malnutrition? This is a sobering moment as I begin to understand that part of our call here is to make sure that children like her have a chance to succeed. Once we have arrived, we are greeted with open arms and hearts at the Children's Home.

The first full day is just that, very full and almost unbearably hot. Pastor M comes down to snap a few pictures of the teachers as the seminar is about to begin. I am already drenched in sweat as I ask her to run back up to the main house for a towel. Surprisingly, the teachers are very receptive to the presentation, which lulls me into a false sense of security and a belief that the whole trip will go smoothly. Lunch is served in midafternoon, and I am very grateful, as my blood sugar is falling, and nausea is setting in. Lunch is rarely served here, yet we are served lunch every day.

We discuss plans for the compound and school over the next few hours. An additional need is raised during our discussion, which turns out to be an ominous prediction of what is about to occur. Cholera is beginning to surface here in Fond Doux, and therefore outhouses need to be dug along Route #2. After the meeting ends, we climb to the top of the compound property; it is so beautiful there, far from the reality of life below. As we pass the chicken coop, I ask about the egg production and learn that the hens are still not laying eggs. They have purchased *Raising Chickens for Dummies*, which causes us to laugh but also urges Pastor M to read the entire book in the course of twenty-four hours. Our final stop is the compound reservoir, and I am happily surprised by how secure it is.

We stop to visit the American missionary and one of the founders on our way down. He and Pastor M hit it off immediately. He recounts numerous stories from his thirty-eight years of missionary work in Haiti. Tears are flowing from Pastor M's eyes as we descend the stairs. I jokingly tell her that we cannot forget the tissues on our next visit. After dinner, we hear the music from the church begin; no one from the main house is going, and although I would like to attend, my body is not willing.

Saturday begins with an important meeting where the final estimate for the school floor will be negotiated. After a grueling three-hour meeting of measuring and calculating, the meeting ends with no resolution. We decide to postpone our final decision and take the children to the beach, allowing Pastor M her first chance to plant her feet in the real Haiti among the shanties. Seeing poverty from the safety of a moving air-conditioned vehicle and standing in the middle of it are two very different experiences. The children hit the water for an hour or so while we soak in the irony of such atrocious poverty alongside the majesty and beauty of God's creation. The beach has a strong fecal smell again today and is literally one big toilet; however, with no public sanitation, the people who live here have few choices.

Once we're back on the compound, a rain shower cools the air temporarily, making it a perfect time to walk and visit Ronny, the little boy with Down syndrome. I am overjoyed to see that he is now worm-free and in good health. I still have a haunting feeling that on one of these mission trips I will learn that he has starved to death; I pray that I am wrong. We find his mom passed out on a concrete porch. I have never seen anyone sleeping facedown on concrete before, and it seems highly peculiar to me.

We spend the rest of our day loving on and playing with the compound children. Whenever we are out of our room, they are with us. The number of children on the compound seems to fluctuate hourly, which explains why we cannot get a definitive answer as to how many children the compound supports.

Sunday morning I am up early and expectant for a special touch by the Holy Spirit. No one else is ready, and Pastor M doesn't want to be late, so we walk down to the church by ourselves; I should have known better. The pastor sees us in the pews and ushers us on stage to be honored guests. As we comply, I am becoming anxious and slightly hyperventilating, but soon we are lost in praise and worship, oblivious to being on display.

As we sit in preparation for the message, the Holy Spirit keeps bringing Ephesians 2:10 to my mind; moments later I am asked to speak. Fear and adrenaline are trying to consume me until I speak, and the Holy Spirit takes over, explaining the implications of this scripture for the Body of Christ in Haiti. As I return to my seat, I silently thank the Holy Spirit for taking over. Attendance is light, perhaps only a third of the normal Sunday attendees, but I have no idea why.

The afternoon is spent playing with the children and relaxing. As dinner approaches, we receive news that one of the school's children has died of cholera. The superintendent of the school is with us and noticeably shaken. I remember all too well the shock and hollow feelings that overwhelm when one of your students dies. We lay hands on her and pray; soon she appears better. Dinner is a somber occasion as word arrives that another churchwoman has died, followed shortly by news of another death at the foot of the compound border. It is now on our doorstep, and everyone is feeling vulnerable. The decision is made that all children within the compound border will spend the night. Teams are assembled at the church to go door to door and find the sick. Finally, good news! As they were zipping the second grader's body bag, she began to breathe again. God had resurrected her, and she eventually made a full recovery.

The final day begins with the last teacher seminar, and it is once again well received. The superintendent asks me to stay and speak with the principal. I explain the rotating schedule and its necessity. He is very unhappy when he leaves, as am I. He is second in command and needs to be on board with the changes being instituted. As we begin our goodbyes, we stop to place a hedgerow of protection around the compound and cover it with the blood of Jesus. There is so much to do here that I do not want to leave. Tears fill my eyes as I hug each of the children and say goodbye.

Once back in Port-au-Prince, we drive by Cité Soleil, the worst slum in the northern hemisphere. It is a shantytown of epic proportions, not only dirty but surrounded by water on three sides. The UN oversees this area with automatic weapons wielded high above the streets atop cement walls covered in razor wire. I say that I would not want to get out here, and I am told I would not be allowed to.

I am not prepared for the gravity of what I am about to witness next. As we continue our drive toward Canaan, blue dots appear on the horizon. The whole mountainside is littered with ragtag tents as far as we are able to see. I am left speechless by the magnitude of the poverty as we drive five miles across its length and an additional two miles to cover its width. Compared to the city tent villages, this is relatively spacious; however, what is gained in space is lost in accessibility. It is way too far to walk to the city and there is neither water nor food nor any place to buy them and no hope for a job. These people are completely dependent upon mission aid.

We reach our lodging just before dusk and enjoy a quiet meal. Afterward, we find women holding babies while sitting Indian style on the ground. They have the children wrapped in both their arms and legs. We learn that this is a technique used to comfort traumatized children when they first arrive. The children are from the tent city orphanage, and their stomachs are hard and distended from malnutrition.

Later we join in the praise and worship and stay for a short film. A little boy named Kevin asks my name and then disappears in the crowd of children. He soon returns with a small cup of popcorn and slides himself onto my lap, where, except for slapping the two girls in front of us, he remains for the remainder of the evening. We are told that the children choose an adult and stay with them for the duration of their stay. Perhaps this is a mechanism of hope that someone will someday fall in love with them and take them home. After a long, hot, sleepless night, we begin our journey home—both of us now committed to doing whatever we can to help Haiti's children.

As you can now discern, it did not take us long to fall in love with Haiti and her people. We thought we knew so much at the time, but God has continued to show us how little we knew and how far we still have to go. As our lessons progress, I would like you to take note of the prophetic words that God delivered and the fulfillment of those words in subsequent letters. I have ordered our lessons chronologically so that you may discover our development, our frailties, and the methods by which God instructed us. We all have our own journeys to follow to become more and more like Jesus, knowing we will never reach this goal until He brings us to our eternal home. Nevertheless, my heart's desire is to hear the words, "Well done, good and faithful servant," once I reach my final destination. Blessings to you both!

In His love,

Pastor D

My Dearest Macy and Mark,

I am so sorry to hear that your midterm exam results were not up to your expectations. I know you both put everything you had into preparing for them. Perhaps it was not effort you were lacking; rather, the method of study you used may have been lacking. May I suggest not only stepping out of the box, but also throwing the box away?

Early in my university studies, I found myself in Chemistry 1. I had slept through high school chemistry and was sorely lacking any base of knowledge. I prepared for the first test with hours of tedious study, only to completely tank the first exam. My first instinct was to give up because obviously I was not going to succeed. The Holy Spirit quickened me to the nature of such lies and I began to examine why I did so poorly. I knew every answer on the test; however, I was too slow and could not finish the exam in the prescribed time limit. I began to practice each problem with a stopwatch and continued to practice until I could do each problem in a matter of seconds rather than minutes. The result was that I never again received a mark lower than an A in any chemistry class I took throughout my studies.

You are going to fail and get knocked down and even injured; what matters is what you do next. I have stumbled and fallen innumerable times; yet each time I fall, He picks me up and brushes me off. In Genesis, we learn about Jacob. It is easy to focus solely on his loves and his children; however, his early story shows him to be a liar, a con artist, and a fraud; yet God called him, chose him, and blessed him. Let's face it; Jacob was loaded with human frailties and flaws. God redeemed Jacob through his weaknesses, not in spite of them.

Each of our lessons is associated with extremely vivid memories of the faces of the people that compose them. Each face still engenders an emotional response in me. Some faces cause me to smile and feel comforted or loved, while others evoke sorrow, sadness, or tears. Although I have changed all the names of those who have served with us, nevertheless I will endeavor to conjure and allude to the feelings that they generate within me as I continue with your discipleship.

Lesson 3: Embrace Your Foibles and Failures

The Four Horsemen

Once again, we board the plane and fly off, leaving the comforts of home behind, and before us lies the unknown! I have my plan in hand and my walls raised, guarding my heart from the pain and despair that await us. One of my favorite paraphrased quotes is from C. T. Studd: Some want to live within the sound of a chapel bell; I wish to run a rescue mission within a yard of Hades. Little do we know how apropos and prophetic this saying will be, both for this trip and for our eventual mission post.

This is our home church pastor's first and only trip to Haiti, and he will be preaching two services. Pastor M will be planting the garden and making sure that the composting project has begun. I will be observing the school and holding two seminars for the teachers. I am aware that although we have an itinerary, God may have other plans. I have prayed for God's will to be accomplished on this trip; someday I will be smart enough to be prepared when I pray such prayers.

As we weave through the city, I comment on how clean it appears; this brings an immediate smile to my face as I remember how strange that comment sounded when I heard it on my first trip here. I wonder how our pastor is processing what he sees as we pull over for our usual grocery stop. Suddenly we hear shots as three men run into the parking lot, followed by five Haitian police officers carrying automatic weapons. One of the men resists, and they strike him repeatedly in the head with the butts of their weapons. As we pull out of the parking lot into the mire of traffic and bodies, we see that he is still bleeding, handcuffed, and placed in the back of a police pickup truck. (An interesting and amusing side note here: the women on our team took cover behind the cement pillars in the store as the men stood mesmerized by the scene unfolding in the parking lot. I guess this proves who is more rational.)

Soon our pastor is no longer speaking. I realize he is experiencing emotional overload and is unable to absorb any more pain. I stop my running commentary as I surmise that this is a common reaction when witnessing Satan's slave market for the very first time. We are once again warmly greeted as we arrive at the Children's Home, and I feel as though we have arrived at home. We eat a good meal, enjoy the evening's church service, and settle in for a welcome night's sleep after a long day of travel.

Each day here is very full; we have so much to accomplish and so little time to fulfill our mission. The feeding kitchen has a new manager, and the quality of the food has vastly improved, which makes me quite happy, considering that many of the children will only receive this meal daily. While I present the first seminar to the teachers, the rest of the team heads to Locul at the compound's beach property. I am convinced that everyone who comes with us should experience planting their feet in the middle of a shantytown because of the powerful and lasting memories it creates. Pastor M is delighted to see that an old blind man she treated during the last medical clinic is doing so well.

There is a four-month-old baby sitting on the ground being supervised by a three-year-old. This is the norm here where babies raise babies. One seldom sees adult supervision or even affection toward children, which seems peculiar because they are quite loving and affectionate toward us. Soon the baby pitches forward and face-plants in the dirt. It is obvious that the baby is struggling, but no one moves to assist the little one. Our pastor picks her up and holds his first child victim of Haiti's atrocious poverty.

The team pulls out bubbles, and shortly there are fifty or so children chasing bubbles along the beach. The children receive presents from America, and the older ones are quite fond of the sunglasses and hats. One naked little girl has used a red canvas bag as her dress. The picture of her wearing this bag has become one of my favorite depictions of child poverty in Haiti. The day ends with another service where our pastor delivers his final message that is both timely and relevant for the needs of the congregation.

The next morning begins early as our pastor's time is already finished; little do we know that the timing of his departure is completely orchestrated by the Holy Spirit. The seminar for the teachers goes smoothly and seems to be well received. We eat a good lunch, and just as everything seems right, the day takes a drastic turn for the worse. I've been lulled into an ephemerally placid state of complacency, or else I would have felt the arrival of "the Horsemen." Word comes in that one of the male church members has died of a mysterious fever. The mood turns somber among the team; however, the Haitians seem to take the news in stride. During the past summer's cholera outbreak, twelve members of the church passed away. Death is an everyday occurrence here, part of life.

Soon word comes in that there is a baby in need of rescue. Pastor M, the young teacher I have been mentoring, and I begin to hunt for the child. Apparently, the mother had left the child with an invalid neighbor while she went to PaP, never to return. Murder, kidnapping, rape, and sexual and domestic slavery are all very real here; we will never know this side of heaven what happened to her.

We frantically search from shack to shack until a little boy leads us to the baby. We find her lying in the dirt covered in feces with insects crawling all over her. Pastor M is undeterred by the stench and horrid sight; she grabs a towel off of a nearby clothesline, wraps the baby in it, and runs back to the main house with the baby cradled in her arms. The baby emerges some time later bathed, dressed, and with her hair cutely braided. She is nine months old but looks more like a three-month-old due to the ravages of malnutrition. Her lower leg is the circumference of my middle finger, and as I run my fingers over her gums, teeth have yet to appear. Her name is Lilly, and she begins to doze off as the American founder agrees to raise her. I pray she flourishes until we are able to see her once again.

Night falls as "the Horsemen" tighten their grip. We learn that one of the school's teachers has been sick for a while. The Holy Spirit quickens Pastor M, and she asks if we may see her. We enter her room to offer prayer, unprepared for what we see. Her face is expressionless, and her eyes appear to be sunken in her head. She is little more than a bag of bones as I take her temperature, which is approaching one hundred and five degrees. She looks like the poster child for Ebola. I mix a fifty percent alcohol and cool water solution that Pastor M applies to the major areas of blood flow. This solution has never failed me until this night. Her fever begins to fall and then jets upward once again. "The Horsemen" are closing in, and I fear that if we cannot break her fever, she will be dead by morning.

As we rummage through her medications, I find an unopened bottle of Tylenol. I ask when the last time fever-reducing medication was administered to her. We were told that she had never been given any. I administer 1000 mgs of Tylenol before we leave to intercede for her. We separately find quite places to pray. A level of minor travail overtakes me, and pain courses through my whole body as I pray and cry out to the Lord. Within an hour, the Lord answers, and the burden lifts from both of us simultaneously. Pastor M goes to check on her and returns smiling: the fever has broken.

The heaviness of the previous day has passed away by morning. I preach the message that God gives me, and my nervousness turns to boldness as the Holy Spirit works through me to deliver God's Word. Later that day we begin discussing the adoption of one of the children who is getting close to us and vice versa. We know we must put our faith in God as He leads us on this incredible journey of service for His glory. Weary, but encouraged, we begin our journey back to the first world where obliviousness and self-absorption are the order of the day.

The eventual outcomes of this journey are not what we hoped and prayed for. Lilly was suffering from severe malnutrition, malaria, and typhoid. We were too late to stop the damage that had already occurred in her young brain. She is a bundle of joy and smiles, but she is now a special needs child. The teacher never fully recovered, as the staff had to pray her back from death's precipice on two other occasions. Finally, her witchdoctor mother removed her from the compound and its divine protection; she died shortly afterward. We never adopted the little girl; my heart still grieves over what this child endured. It would be easy to view these events as futile failures; however, what we learned allowed us to help many other children simply because we were now wiser and more experienced. I pray that as I share our failures, you will learn from us and not have to endure such pain.

In His love,
Pastor D

My Dearest Macy and Mark,

One of my greatest joys and responsibilities is to make sure I pass on what God has taught me. Discipleship and mentoring are crucial components of missionary life. When I was in high school, I ran track. My coaches could never understand why I was so much faster in the four by one hundred meter relay than I was in the open one hundred meter. I ran the first leg of the relay; thus there was no running start involved. I understood the reason the whole time. My teammates were also my friends, and I did not want to let them down. Because of this, I was able to dig deeper into myself and in turn run faster.

This is very much like discipleship. We as missionaries have the honor and duty to train our disciples to the best of our ability. The eventual outcome should be that we work ourselves out of a job. In essence, we pass the baton after running our best leg of the race. Every relay race must begin somewhere; this is how our discipleship race began.

Lesson 4: Discipleship

A New Dawn

Bags in hand, we must run the last hundred yards to our gate. Our plane has boarded, and the doors are about to shut, but praise be to God because He has a mission for us, and He will not be denied. As we settle into our seats, I see expectancy mixed with a tinge of fear on our team's faces.

This is our first opportunity to bring my students on a mission trip. I realize that this will be a long arduous day so I take a deep breath and relax until the plane begins its descent and my students' heads are bobbing and weaving straining to see Haiti appear on the horizon. On the ground, our transition through the airport is seamless.

Pastor M and our teacher intern stuff themselves into the back of the loaded truck as we begin our journey. I am not happy with this arrangement, but we are short on money, and I am keenly aware of the perils we may face. If we are not careful, we may overload the girls before ever reaching our compound. We decide that this would be a good time to tour PaP. We take a different route through Cité Soleil, which gives me a better idea of the size of this massive slum. Still miles from Canaan, the blue dots begin to appear on the distant mountainside. *Click, click, click* is all that can be heard as the girls snap multiple pictures of what they are witnessing. We pass Cité Soleil again on our way back, but this time we drive very slowly so we can easily view the most putrid, trash-strewn water surrounding this massive shantytown. The least bit of rain can begin the all-too-common flooding here. The suffering and violence are of demonic proportions and conjure images in my brain of what the Lake of Fire must be like. Our final stop is the National Palace, which was destroyed during the earthquake.

After snapping a few more pictures, we head toward our compound.

The girls are beginning to nod off, and I decide to stop my running commentary and switch places so Pastor M can ride up front. She refuses because she always puts the needs of others above her own, insisting that our intern take the front seat. The smells and constant jostling she has received in the truck bed have already beaten up my wife. The rest of the drive is also rough and unpleasant, with waves of nausea gripping us both as the scenery whizzes by. The cap of the truck is open to assist airflow, but it also allows layers of dirt and diesel exhaust to pile on us.

Sore but intact, we arrive at the compound. The weariness of travel immediately turns to joy as the children run screaming to greet us. They begin chanting our intern's name, which makes me happy since she has sacrificed so much to be their English teacher for the year. My students' faces are all smiles as the children hug them one by one. After settling into our rooms, I ask Pastor M if she is ready to see Lilly. We peer into her room and see a beautiful new crib, but no baby. She is with the white missionary founder who has completely taken over her care. We introduce the team, and they take to him immediately. As I cradle her in my arms, my thoughts go to my granddaughter, praying that this little one will be loved as much. She now has two teeth and can support her own weight, although her belly is still hard. She has nearly doubled in size since we last saw her three months ago.

Supper is good, and we are all full as I ask about responses to my unanswered emails. The superintendent has been sick and so has not read any of them. She has scheduled the teachers' in-service training for Wednesday and Thursday mornings. My schedule is now totally broken, but I have been to Haiti enough times to realize the necessity of being flexible. We end the evening with our first team meeting, where I happily discover that everyone is holding up well. I decide we will attempt a hot dog feeding at the beach property in Locul the next morning. I distribute money for the food, and we all turn in for the evening.

I am up before 5:00 a.m. every day enjoying the peace and serenity. Once breakfast is served, we drive to Locul to set up for the hot dog feeding. We rope off an area to separate us from the children, and Pastor M does a quick head count while I light the charcoal. There are already 125 children lined up to be fed. We cross the ropes to bring my students, Sela and Hannah, to the beach; they never do make it to the water. They are surrounded by children desperate for attention, and smilingly they oblige each one. One picture of this scene is picked up by the media and makes it halfway around the world. I scan the crowd of children, looking for guinea worms or their scars along with blond heads that may signal malnutrition.

By the time the food is prepared the crowd of children has more than doubled in size. We only bought three hundred hot dogs and I am concerned that we may run out. Everyone jumps into action as Pastor M cooks, I place the hotdogs on bread and apply ketchup, while Hannah and Sela deliver them to the children. We all work quickly and tirelessly until all the hot dogs are gone; unfortunately, there are still forty children who have not been fed, and they begin to cry out for food. Sela is overwhelmed and begins to weep. She is the first but not the last to release her emotional overload caused by conditions in Haiti. We take her aside and explain that there are three hundred children with full bellies because we came. I scan the team's faces and decide that it is time for us to leave.

We assess the compound children's math skills in the afternoon. Their skills range from very good to atrociously bad. I am somewhat at a loss as to why one of the obviously brighter children is struggling. Our intern tells us that she failed the English midterm even though she speaks the best English. The Holy Spirit brings an idea forth in my mind. I create manipulatives and retest her in math as well as administering the English midterm verbally. She scores 100 percent on each test, so I ask to see her written work. Many of her letters are written backwards, and I surmise she has dyslexia. We next begin a birthday party to celebrate Lilly's first birthday. She is passed around and loved on before we dig into her cake. Pastor M has brought food and clothing as presents for her, and I see a special connection forming between them. As long as we are involved with Haiti, Lilly has a guardian angel in my wife.

During that evening, we held a meeting with the founders that I had been forewarned about. We were all about bringing life to Haiti, and God had impressed that deeply within my heart, changing urgency into wisdom, which prompted us to slow down and learn more about the

Haitian culture. Americans most often exude cockiness, believing that our way is the only way and certainly the best way to do ministry.

During this process of helping, we had created some walls barricaded by bruised feelings and egos. This meeting attempted to scale those walls and begin the process of tearing them down. We spoke first, expressing our feelings of love and admiration for what was taking place here at the compound. Each person spoke in turn graciously and respectfully.

One of the founders and clan leader spoke last. Although he also spoke lovingly and graciously, the pain, anger, and frustration over the events of the last year were apparent. The Holy Spirit had prepared me for his need to vent, and through it all, understanding between us began to sprout. Relationships are always a work in progress, but this evening was a good step in the right direction. The evening concluded with a very intense team meeting with tears flowing all around. I immediately made a decision to lighten our itinerary for the next day, realizing that the Holy Spirit might have other plans.

The final meetings with the teachers were frustrating, to say the least. Every time I attempted to make progress on the agenda, they would lead me down another rabbit hole. Outwardly, I was patient and understanding, making sure that I filled each rabbit hole before proceeding to the next agenda item. At one point, the superintendent became irritated and began yelling at the principal, who was the main culprit in slowing our agenda. I had been pouring as much as possible into the superintendent, and I was very proud of how she stood up to him. Although she was his boss, it is very uncommon for a woman to put a man in his place in Haiti. Her growth as an administrator and leader was both apparent and encouraging. Unwittingly, these teacher meetings were helping our intern as well. She was becoming frustrated with the teachers and their unwillingness to change, especially when it came to corporal punishment. As we unpacked each day's events in our team meetings, she began to understand the bigger picture.

The rest of the day was spent hiking and playing with the children. It was wonderful watching everyone simply play. Pastor M met a boy named Stephan, who had recently moved into the area. He was loaded with worms and unable to attend school because he had moved midway through the year. The other children also ostracized him because the scarring from the worms had temporarily disfigured his face. After worming him, Pastor M and I agreed to pay for a private tutor for him as well as the young girl with dyslexia. We had discussed adopting her and bringing her back to the States. It was painful when we realized that we would not be able to adopt her. Although she is in third grade in Haiti, she would have only tested into first grade in the States and would not be able to graduate from high school before reaching the maximum age. I believed God would intervene; however, He chose to work on my heart instead. We were going to help the compound children right here in Haiti. I believed that I had made it through the week unscathed, but I was wrong as the reality of not adopting her sent tears of sorrow streaming down my face. She was so upset the night before we left that I felt as if my heart was being ripped from my chest as we embraced her and tried to comfort her.

The night before we left, I preached a message on God's armor. I believe that our Haitian brothers and sisters must know how to defend themselves from the constant onslaught of spiritual attacks here. Our last team meeting was also filled with tears, as no one was ready to leave. Our shared experiences brought the team closer together and helped everyone deal with their emotions. I am so proud of how this team came together and served.

I was hoping that this mission would be a life-changing experience for Sela and Hannah; I believe God answered that prayer. Before this trip, both girls were marginally Catholic, but each said the sinner's prayer and accepted Jesus as their Lord and Savior upon returning home. They in essence were the pioneers who allowed me to develop future teams as well as youth discipleship training and mentorship. What their bravery made possible is evidenced in my writings and advice to you. It is all about passing the baton!

In His love

Pastor D

My Dearest Macy and Mark,

There are times in the field when God will make you intentionally uncomfortable. This is not purely a physical occurrence, although many times it is. For me, it tends to be emotional distress; God blessed me with an exceptional IQ, but perhaps only an average EQ. He has constantly tested and stretched me in emotional ways, helping me grow in many areas. The following mission forced me to overcome both physical and emotional stress. These baby steps were of the utmost necessity, preparing us for a life of foreign service, and with each small victory God showed His glory and majesty. In retrospect, the accumulation of each baby step is what allows us to be able to minister in any type of situation and environment. Each step was so infinitesimally small that it took years to realize how far we had progressed.

Lesson 5: Character Supersedes Comfort

Mirage

I begin this trip with mixed emotions, hidden agendas, and a heavy heart. Distractions and fatigue composed the pre-trip attacks. I feel unfocused and disconnected, a dangerous combination when leading a team of unfamiliar faces. I place this trip in God's hands because I am incapable of leading. The itinerary, usually impeccably thought out and calculated, has changed so many times that only God knows what this trip will hold.

Once settled into our rooms at the compound, we hold our first team meeting, which breaks the ice and helps me take ownership of the team. Unbeknownst to me, our team nurse is struggling and wants to leave. We decide that we will feed the children of Locul the first full day. This is a good team building activity that we have done several times before; thus, I am somewhat confident this outreach will go smoothly. We are getting better at organizing and protecting the teams from potential problems. We are now roping off the beach property and line the children on the beach. As each child receives a hot dog, they are escorted out the front gate. This prevents congestion and gives us a better head count of the children we have yet to feed; however, some of the older kids run around and get back in line, which has made it necessary for us to mark the back of their hands. I purchased four hundred and fifty hot dogs, and we prayed that we would not run out. We are able to feed every child and bless the caretaker and his family with the leftovers. His youngest daughter, Patricia, has become one of my favorite children on the beach.

That afternoon we did a door-to-door outreach, delivering food and offering prayer in the village of Morose. I had been dreading this event, feeling I might come across like a traveling salesman or an '80s Bible-thumping evangelist preaching fire and brimstone rather than love, grace, and mercy. Within a few minutes, it became apparent that my fear was simply a device of the enemy meant to deter me from what would become one of my favorite types of outreach.

For several months preceding this trip, I had yearned to become more like one of the apostles. As we weaved through the millet fields, our entourage grew. Children appeared from seemingly everywhere, following us from home to home, intently listening as we prayed, playfully laughing, and holding our hands between homes. We blessed people with food, prayed for their needs, and brought them the gifts of repentance, salvation, and healing. I knew this was what Jesus's apostles did and that God had answered my prayer. God had turned my fear into an incredible blessing.

We finished the day with an awesome service at the compound church. Praise and worship were wonderful, and Pastor M preached her first message on forgiveness, which the Lord had given her. She showed no nervousness, just confidence in the word that the Lord had given her. The message was clear and delivered with the passion and heart only my wife possesses. Tears mixed with pride filled my eyes as three of our compound girls melted my heart as they sang praises to the Lord. They are learning English rapidly, which furthers and hastens our bonding. The evening concluded with a team meeting that meshed us closer together.

The next morning was extremely ambitious as we assessed the school progress, painted the mission trailer, worked on electric, and prepared for the afternoon's medical clinic. The organization of the afternoon's outreaches was brilliant. The people entered the medical clinic in the compound church, were then funneled into the school for clothing distribution, and exited the school to be fed. It was an incredible day, but as I looked at the team, I saw exhaustion in their faces. I decided that our Haitian team would set up the next day's clinic and allow the team to rest until they were needed.

I was back to my normal routine the next morning, enjoying a peaceful time with the Lord as the sun began to emerge. Once the clinic at Locul began, we operated six stations: a gate manager, a worming station, two triage stations, a nurse's station, and finally a prayer chair. Each station was staffed with two team members and a translator, which allowed four hundred people to be treated within four hours. The rest of the afternoon was spent hiking on the mountain behind the compound and enjoying God's beautiful creation. The following day the team went to Taino beach in Grand Goave while I fought through dysentery and fever. The enemy tried to deter me from preaching on first Corinthians chapter thirteen that evening, but with God's help, I was able to deliver the message. As I preached, the fever and dysentery left my body and praise be to God, I was completely healed.

The next morning I learned that Jazmine had been sold by her father. She was one of the girls who played frequently on the compound and had spent time with Sela and Hannah three months earlier. I sent out a search party to find the father and double whatever price he was paid; unfortunately, he had left the area, and we never did discover her fate. I have never healed from the events of this day, and visions of Jazmine bound in domestic and sexual slavery have frequented many a dream. As I researched the Haitian *restavek*s (child slaves), I learned that 225,000 children were estimated to be currently enslaved in Haiti. Nothing I had ever experienced had made me feel as helpless as I did at that moment.

One of my personal goals for the trip was to model correct parenting to the Haitians. Discipline must always be balanced with love so the children will seek positive reinforcement rather solely negative reinforcement. I gave more hugs, more kisses, and more encouraging words than ever before. Pastor M and I told numerous children how much we loved them multiple times per day. This was a total leap of faith, bringing me closer than ever before to each child—something that my flesh really did not want to do, given the looming possibility that our mission organization would cease to minister here. A mirage is something illusory, without substance or reality. I believed that was what we were experiencing during the struggle over control of the compound, a matter that God has still yet to resolve.

In His love,

Pastor D

My Dearest Macy and Mark,

When you asked what was the most difficult experience for me, you are touching an area within me that may never heal; however, I will endeavor to answer your question straightaway, although with a modicum of caution because I am not yet sure that you are ready for my answer.

The needless deaths and unnecessary suffering of children are most difficult for me to endure. I wrote the following story because I needed to release the emotional pain concerning ten-year-old Jazmine being sold into slavery. I have never really come to terms with my pain, and I am able to push on simply because I know that I serve a good and sovereign God. Statistics show that most girls die within the first five years of servitude. It has been eight years since Jazmine was sold; this is how I imagine her demise.

Lesson 6: Sovereignty

Baby in a Box

As the morning heat rises, Crystalina's body begins to succumb; only a few minutes old, she does not possess the strength to even cry. She is curled up in a tiny box while the dirt from the streets begins to pile up on her frail newborn body. With all her remaining strength, Crystalina musters one last little scream. It is barely audible, just as Martha is walking past the gate. Martha flings the orphanage gate door open and grabs the box containing Crystalina's fragile body. "Savages" is all she can say as the orphanage gate slams shut once again.

Jazmine's day has started at 4:00 a.m. She brushes the dirt from her one tattered dress as she stretches, arising from the corner of the kitchen floor where she sleeps. Her back is aching, and she is bruised from the nightly violations. She is now nearly full term and she can easily feel Crystalina moving around. She quickly emerges from her master's shanty into the mud- and muck-filled streets of Cité Soleil. She inhales deeply, sucking in the cool morning air, coughing from the stench of feces mingling with rotting garbage. She bends over, and in an instant the charcoal is lit as she pauses to thank God for another day.

She is luckier than many children here are. She hears the toddler crying from the shanty next door. Her mother's milk has long since dried up from lack of nutrition, and she is now on a steady diet of mud cookies, quelling her cries as she slowly starves to death. Jazmine prays that God will take the toddler home soon. Two days ago a five-year-old three doors down died of typhoid fever. She remembers back to last year's cholera outbreak when people were being carried out of here in body bags on a daily basis.

She hustles inside to grab a pot, scraping the scraps from last night's dinner with her fingers; she quickly devours the quarter cup of dried leftovers. This will serve as her one and only meal today. She must consume as many calories as possible in the hope that she will not slip into sickle cell crisis once again. After she has fixed the family breakfast, she helps the girls prepare for school. Finally, they all leave for the day. A quick sweep of the house, and she is off to draw water from the well almost two miles away. This will be her first of five trips to the community well today. Her shoulders are aching. She is uncertain if the pain is from the weight of the water or the welts from the wire her masters beat her with.

Shaking and exhausted from the heat and the weight of the buckets, she pauses to rest. She picks at the Guinea worms surrounding her knees; ripping through the skin with her fingernails, she frees one and pulls it from her body. One less worm, one more scar, but a trade she gratefully makes.

She drifts off in thought to the day her life changed forever. She and her mother were bathing outside when an argument with a man broke out. Enraged, the man cut her mother's left arm completely off, sliced halfway through the other, and left long slashes on her back and inner thighs. A kind missionary woman rushed her to the hospital to see and pray for her mom, but it was too late. Her lifeless, mutilated body was left strewn on the table. The doctors had been unable to stop the massive blood loss caused by her wounds.

Two weeks later, Hurricane Matthew devastated southern Haiti; Jazmine's dad was one of the victims. The horrific odor of decomposing flesh preceded the box trucks full of trash and human bodies. Limbs were protruding all throughout the trash. Dangling from one of the limbs was a silver chain and locket containing the picture of their once happy family. After this, she moved in with her aunt and uncle, but shortly thereafter, her aunt fell ill. Over the next few months, she watched helplessly as HIV ravaged her aunt's body. It was shortly after the passing of her aunt that Jazmine's uncle sold her into slavery as a restavek for $150—a price that nearly doubles the world average.

She is brought out of her thoughts as her water breaks, gushing down her legs into the dirt. She decides then and there that her baby will not suffer her same fate. She sets out, walking through the day and into the night, fighting the quickening and intensifying contractions. She makes it to an alley just in sight of the orphanage. Here she brings Crystalina into the world. She places her in a box and then leaves her on the steps of the orphanage. She is still bleeding and so weak that the world begins to spin. She lies atop a pile of cardboard; just before she closes her eyes, she hears Crystalina's cry. Jazmine opens her eyes to the embrace of her savior. As Jazmine's earthly story ends; thus, the story of Crystalina begins.

> Only one life, 'twill soon be past;
> Only what's done for Christ will last.
> — C. T. Studd

I must apologize for the brutality of this story. In reality, I have absolutely no idea what happened to Jazmine once she was sold. I do know that I am not sovereign, not the savior, and certainly not Superman. The elements of Jazmine's story are not solely hers; however, most of them had happened to the five young girls we took into our home to raise. Sovereignty is an issue that must not be overlooked. If you even for a moment think you are in control, then be prepared for a very hard fall.

In His love,

Pastor D

My Dearest Macy and Mark,

I am so happy and proud that you have completed your first semester. What thrills me most is that you are about to undertake your first short-term missions trip. I understand your reservations concerning this trip; you have committed your life to missions, yet you have never left the relative safety of the United States. An unknown place can be scary, leading to anxiety and a severe dread that may impede your progress or even stop it. The unknown should not be viewed in this manner. God is about to teach you something, which should excite you and fill you with anticipation. This does not mean that there will be no heartache; rather, it is a step closer to becoming like Jesus. Enjoy yourselves, and relish the relationships that the Holy Spirit establishes in the field. The following trip really changed me forever. It was full of the unknown and a time when I needed to face many fears as well.

Lesson 7: Usher in the Unknown

Journey to the Mountain of Death

It had been four months since my last trip to Haiti, a longer time away than any other period since we had been going. God had used this time to deal with my heart and to refocus me on His mission. Turning over control of the compound to the nationals hurt me deeply. It seemed the right thing to do, but the fear of not seeing the children and of broken relationships had been weighing heavily on my heart. I professed to have faith, yet when tested, my faith was not as strong as I would have liked.

I remember standing in church and telling God to use me, telling Him that I was not afraid anymore. But before this trip, I had fought nightmares for two weeks. The same questions arose time after time: What would happen if a child died while we were trying to rescue him or her? Would God give me the strength to handle the situation, or would I break? Fear is a peculiar emotion; it causes us to freeze in our tracks and not move forward. This is why it is one of the enemy's favorite devices. Little did I know how many fears I would have to face during this journey.

There was no rest as we began our mission almost immediately upon landing in Port-au-Prince. When we met at the airport, one of the California sorority girls, Lisa, was in the truck. I had mixed feelings upon meeting her. We had several places to take her that morning, but I was anxious to begin our mission. I was also fighting feelings of rivalry and perhaps a little jealousy as well. This sorority was held in high regard at the compound and in the eyes of the children as well. I had always felt a competing spirit as we tried to gain control of everyday operation of the compound. These young women habitually kept the children up late and broke pretty much every rule we had set.

Getting to know Lisa over the next few days was definitely a God encounter. My whole opinion of her and the sorority changed, as God revealed her heart and her efforts on behalf of the Haitian people. She had stayed an extra ten days in Haiti to visit businesses that could potentially become global.

Our first stop was a small factory that made sandals from used tires and old leather. To my surprise, the president of the company greeted us; I had known her as a teenager when her family owned the only decent Italian bakery in West Palm Beach. She and another incredible young woman were supporting twenty families by providing jobs, food, and education for their children. You never know whom God will use!

It was a beautiful morning to begin our first full day in Haiti. I was keenly aware that this was not a vacation, and my spiritual antenna was already up. This trip was purely logistical, and was needed to help determine the direction that God was leading us. I met a Haitian pastor who had grown up as a street kid at the American compound in PaP and now ran multiple ministries in Cité Solei. We began by visiting his compound on the outskirts of Cité Solei. Guards tended the gate as we entered what was an amazingly modern facility. He ran a primary school for four hundred children and had a large church on the property. His feeding program served fifteen hundred children during the school year, but that day it looked like a ghost town. He shared his vision as we began our tour of Cité Solei, the largest ghetto in the western hemisphere and home to more than eight hundred thousand people. As we weaved through the tenement streets, we descended lower and lower into the slum. I felt like a character in Dante's *Inferno* descending through the nine levels of Hades. Progress was slow as we continually waited for the masses of children to clear the road. There were no adults around, only children, some of them as young as two.

We arrived at the worst section, a place so bad that I once said that I would not want to get out here; the response was that I wouldn't be allowed to get out here. As the Haitian pastor pulled over and grabbed a bag of candy for the children, I opened my door and planted my feet in the place I so affectionately call the "Lake of Fire." I was not even the slightest bit concerned or afraid. God had granted me boldness as I walked the streets, taking pictures of the children and the infamous mud cakes. These salad plate sized cakes are exactly what they sound like: mud, with a little sugar and oil. They are sold to families of starving children to fill their stomachs so the children stop crying while they are starving to death. Thousands of these cakes were drying in the sun. I thought that I would have been mad or righteously indignant; however, I found myself quietly sad, and perhaps in awe of the gravity of the plight of these people.

As we slowly ascended from the "Lake of Fire," I thought about the nightly rapes and murders and the disease, parasites, and starvation here, but mostly I thought about the children. As we pulled out onto the main road, my attention was drawn to the haunting contrast of a pretty little girl adorned in a perfectly laundered pink dress walking past the most putrid, littered, and infested body of water I had ever seen. It was then that the Holy Spirit reminded me that the encounters I had with ministries on this trip raised an important question. How well do we play with others? It became obvious as the trip unfolded that all the ministries we were considering for collaboration wanted control. I was uncertain how this would all play out, but I had a feeling deep within that we would be tasked with our own mission.

The next day was a beautiful cool, sunny morning with a nice, steady breeze. The founder of the American orphanage and guesthouse in PaP was speaking with a middle-aged Haitian woman. She was pleading for help, which really grabbed my attention; shortly thereafter, bags of rice appeared. Another guest at the American compound walked over to her and gave her a hundred-dollar bill. The woman did not speak Creole, but fortunately, she also spoke Spanish. I listened to the conversation and discovered that this woman ran an extremely poor orphanage housing ninety children with almost no food.

We had been struggling with which ministry to visit that day, and this seemed like a clear sign that the Holy Spirit had orchestrated our delay. Ten boxes of rice were loaded into her truck and we followed her through the gate. It was about a forty-minute drive to the orphanage, and thirty or so young boys ran to greet us at the gate. I was immediately struck by how close the ages of these children were. As we began our tour of the house, I realized that this house should not really have held more than about twenty children. Each of us grabbed a couple of children to carry with us. There was a unique unpleasant smell to the place that I could not quite identify. The orphanage housed sixty boys and thirty girls; some of the children had special needs.

In one of the boys' rooms, thirty beds were stacked three high with only about eighteen inches between them. The roof was unfinished; thus, they had covered the room with translucent green panels, creating in essence a greenhouse for the boys to sleep in. The temperature was in the mid-nineties, and the boys' room must have easily been a hundred and ten degrees. Much of the house was dark, damp, and musty, with the feel of an old prison. She showed us the office last, where the ten boxes of rice we brought had been stacked in a storage area. I realized from the size of this area that it was reserved for food storage, but the ten boxes we brought were the only food visible. As I walked back to the truck, I noticed a young boy leaning against it. It took a second, but then I noticed he only had one leg. This place was bad, really bad!

Back at the American compound, I told the story of this visit. A woman from California was leaving the next day. She reached into her bag and handed me a hundred-dollar bill. Someone remarked that one hundred and twenty-five dollars would feed them for a week. She reached back into her bag and handed me another twenty-five dollars. I promised to buy them food and bring her a receipt the next morning. As we pulled back up to the poor orphanage, children once again greeted us, but this time they were chanting, "*Manje, manje,*" which means food. They all had pained, frantic looks on their faces, and my heart sank as we unloaded the food. I had purchased extra food with some of the emergency money I brought so the orphanage should have food for about the next two weeks. I posed for a quick picture, and we were off again. I tried without success to wipe what I had seen from my mind; instead, I just buried it for the moment.

The next morning, I was blessed to worship Jesus with the hundred American compound children. It is such a privilege to serve our Lord that I cannot fathom how anyone would not want the blessings I received when I went there. I had been avoiding the children there like the plague. Fresh wounds from dealing with the possibility of losing our own compound children had made me shy away from developing new attachments. It takes a singularity of purpose and direction to work in Haiti. The plethora of problems in just daily existence there make it easy to sink into a quagmire of despair and lose focus. Only under the direction of the Holy Spirit did we have the discernment and the ability to push forward toward God's ultimate plan. I would have loved nothing more than to open a home in the Haitian countryside and raise twenty or so orphans properly and with love, but to do so we would have had to sacrifice the thousands that we helped.

Our time in PaP was finally over, and a day of travel was welcome. We headed for the mountain of death, a place where barely half the children lived to age five. No food, tainted water, parasites, and disease are the norm there. The city had been hot and dusty, with a heavy, oppressive feel. The drive was long and the mountain pass treacherous; much of the time, I looked at the mountain wall so I could not see the rocks skittering from under our tires off the fifteen-hundred-foot cliff inches away from us. God was with us, and we arrived safely around ten that evening. The air was brisk and clean as we fell into bed for the best night's sleep of the trip.

The next morning began early as we were traveling to Cayes LaSalle that day. This was the poorest village with the greatest need. This was where a little boy I had met at the American compound was rescued from, starving and unable to stand from lack of nutrition. He crawled around on all fours like a dog waiting to be shot and put out of his misery. He must have felt as if he had won the Haitian lottery because he was now being treated like a little prince. While we were at the American compound, his father came to visit him; when the boy saw his father, he turned his face away in fear. It was not that the boy was afraid of his father; rather, he was terrified that his father would take him back to the village where he almost died.

Nearly two hours from base camp deep in the mountain jungle, we found Cayes LaSalle, the village that time had forgotten. Fortunately, God had not forgotten His children there. The food had been delayed, which gave us time to speak with some locals in the community brush arbor. After questioning the villagers for about ten minutes, we learned that less than 10 percent of the village knew anything about Jesus. They never ate rice and beans, and when asked how often the children were fed, their answer was disturbing. "When we have food, we feed the children, and when we have no food, we do not." There were about twenty-five hundred people in the area, and more than half were children.

We then visited some houses. One house had been in such bad shape that when it rained the residents had to stand in the back corner. By the time we arrived, it was too late. The house had collapsed and now was a pile of palm fronds and sticks. The family had moved next door with the grandmother, making her tiny house home to fifteen. They slept in shifts, with half of the family sleeping until one and then the other half of the family would take their turn sleeping. The whole family was malnourished, thin, and frail. This was not a good situation, but we had not seen anything yet.

We next drove to the backside of the village (we later learned that this was a separate village called Cafayier), where we were greeted by another group of children. We identified this as the second feeding site location. The children were incredibly thin, and their clothes were torn and tattered. Most were filthy and obviously malnourished. I stood in shock snapping picture after picture, too numb to feel. I watched what unfolded as if I were watching a movie. I could not believe that this was real! I noticed what I thought were two teenage boys with tattered clothes hanging off them; to my surprise, they were girls! They were so malnourished that there were no signs of puberty. I thought about the soldiers going into Auschwitz concentration camp at the end of WWII and wondered if this was similar to what they saw.

We headed back to the other side and realized that the crowd had doubled in size, as the food was then ready to be served. I walked through the crowd snapping numerous pictures of hungry children devouring their rice and beans. I felt a wave of sadness followed by nausea; the pain was surfacing, and I was about to lose it. It was then that God saw my grief and parted the sea of children. There she was, God's little angel, Josie, standing in what seemed like Hades on Earth. She was three years old, and her smile could melt the hardest of hearts. I knew instantly she was the face that would help bring food to Cayes LaSalle. God had touched me and once again broken through the walls I had tried to build against the pain of this land held hostage.

After I snapped a few more pictures of her, she had a medical exam. Her stomach was beginning to bloat, and she was most likely loaded with worms. I prayed that we would be able to bring food in time to save this child. If I could have taken her then and there, I would have. Overall, we removed nine people from the mountain due to severe malnutrition;

two went to the American compound, and the other seven went to the hospital in Les Cayes. I was determined to bring this village the hope of God, clothes, worm medicine, and more food on my next visit to Haiti. Even today, when I close my eyes I still see the faces of the children there, staring back at me with big brown helpless and hopeless eyes. Our God is mighty to save and I know He has mercy for these children.

As we headed back toward base camp, we passed a teenage boy with no legs lying in the dirt at the foot of his property. We told him that we could not do anything now, but we would bring him a wheelchair on our next visit. That night was much hotter than the last, and it was very difficult to fall asleep.

The next day we traveled to Pestel and then on to Billard, (pronounced Bea), which is the largest city in the area, with only one doctor to serve more than eighty thousand people. I have to admit I was a little disappointed. Although the hilly narrow streets and pastel colors reminded me a little of an Italian fishing village, it was almost as poor and dirty as the mountains. It was market day, and we were hurried up a set of steep cement stairs with no railings. Our bags were stacked behind the stairs, and security was placed there to guard them. I am such an avid movie fan that my mind seemed to be making connections between what I was experiencing and movie scenes, probably because I had no frame of reference for what I encountered on this trip. I say this because the day before, I had felt like Sean Connery in *Medicine Man*, scouring the Amazon, but as I walked up these stairs, I might have been in a scene from *Miami Vice*. We were led out to a covered porch with three foot cement walls. The room was divided into three sections separated only by furniture. To the far right were three sets of bunk beds, in the middle a long table and chairs, and to the left a living room arrangement, which was where we waited. The air was hot and still and we were very uncomfortable. I felt exposed, surrounded by all the adjoining rooftops; this would be a perfect location for a sniper to zero in on me.

An hour or so passed, and we were then hurried down the stairs and through the jammed market. The pace at which we were rushed through the market added to my anxiety, which climaxed when I saw our boat. It looked like a big Haitian dugout canoe with a fifteen-horsepower engine. Fear gripped me. I would not normally go out on a lake in a boat this size, let alone head out into the open ocean. The boat was being dashed against the dock by rough seas. I thought about telling everyone that I would see them when they got back, but I sensed the Holy Spirit saying to me, "I've got you." Still, I tried not to listen. *Come on, God,* I silently prayed. *I dealt with my fear of heights and reckless driving, and I walked through Hades. Please don't make me do this.* The only response was that still, small voice saying, "I've got you."

They attempted to hold the boat still as we climbed in. There were no lifejackets in sight, and I was still slightly hyperventilating as we pulled away from the dock. Water crashed into the boat as we pulled out into the bay. Within a minute, I was thoroughly drenched but somehow more at ease. Soon I felt like I was in an episode of *Lost* as all signs of humanity had disappeared during the course of the forty-minute boat ride. We finally pulled into a small cove at the foot of a mountain.

The pastor and about twenty children were waiting there to greet us. One by one, we were shuttled ashore in dugout canoes. We then began the climb up the mountain. I climbed quickly, and soon I was several hundred yards ahead of the group. I turned around to catch my breath and saw a picture that reminded me of the movie *Out of Africa*. The founder of the American compound was being escorted up the mountain caravan style. Someone was holding an umbrella over her head as two others assisted her over every rock. She was the "Great White Hope" there in those mountains. Everyplace we went in Haiti, people knew her. She always gave credit to Jesus, because as we all know, He is the only hope for all of us.

Once at the top we again entered a brush arbor, and the same scenario of feeding and snapping pictures took place. The children looked a little better here. Please do not misconstrue that statement; these people were still in very bad shape. However, by comparison with those at Cayes LaSalle, they were cleaner, healthier, and generally a little better fed. This was probably due to the ocean supplying needed protein in the way of fish. As the children ate, we were led over the hill to the village center. I had to hold back tears when I saw the feast they had prepared for us. Thirty feet of linen-covered tables were packed with food. They had nearly nothing; yet they prepared all they had for us. No one wanted to eat their food, but not to eat would have been offensive. The coffee was incredible, the best I had ever had, infused with cinnamon; it barely needed sugar because it was so smooth. We left quickly after our meal because we had another stop, and our second dinner was being prepared in Pestel.

We hugged the shoreline on our way to the next village. It was brutally hot, and everyone was tired by the time we reached the next dock. The village pastor said it was just up the hill and around the bend; thus, almost everyone made the trek. When a Haitian tells you it is just up the hill and around the bend, it's like telling you that they will be there in 15 minutes. An hour later, we finally reached the village. My hands were getting tight as my blood pressure was climbing from the heat, physical exertion, and lack of water. We spent about fifteen minutes checking out the village children and then headed back. Finally, we made it back to the boat and Pestel for a lobster dinner. We learned that there would also be dinner at base camp and that we should take that into consideration. I had mixed feelings as I forced down my third dinner in as many hours. We were visiting starving babies, and I was so full that I could barely eat breakfast the next day. Something was wrong with this picture. How could we who had so much be so selfish as not to share our blessings with a dying world?

Once off the mountain, I returned to the relative safety of our compound. My first day was difficult there; I was very emotionally closed, and the children seemed distant. I tried writing in my journal to begin the healing process, but I was unable to force even a single word onto paper. God granted me a measure of peace and comfort on the second day as the founders of the compound told me that they would like us to still consider this our home in Haiti and continue to do ministry there. The past was behind us, and we needed to move forward. A sense of relief overtook me, and I felt as if a huge weight had been lifted from my shoulders. The children and I rebounded, and we grew closer than ever before. I had a few people to give money to and needed to enroll a child in school, but for the most part the work was over, and the healing began in earnest. We went to the beach the next two days, and I had a blast playing with the children. Saying goodbye was never an easy task, but I felt much better knowing that we were still welcome at what was once our compound.

One of Brandon Heath's songs says, "Give Me Your Eyes." I used to pray that prayer, but not anymore. Now I pray to see what the Lord wants me to see. As I settled back into life in the first world, I knew that I was changed. I was no longer a "Chocolate Soldier," leading fluff trips so people could say they'd gone to Haiti. It is not my intention to seem harsh because I was once in need of fluff; rather, there is life and death work that needs to be accomplished. Who knows who will be called? Normally there are only two responses to Haiti mission trips: either people will never return, or they will want to come back to help. I believed that we were being called to step up to a higher level. I was more committed than ever to see feeding programs in the remote mountain villages. *Bondye beni ou* (God bless you), my little children, until we are together again.

As you can see, God's intent was not to make me afraid or give me nightmares; rather, it was to create a boldness that I never knew existed within me and to create a resolve for His mission that was much greater than any I had ever experienced. My prayer for you on this trip is that God do the same for you! You can trust Him because He is worthy of your trust! I look forward to reading about your adventure. Be blessed, and bless all those He gives you.

In His love,

Pastor D

My Dearest Macy and Mark,

Regret is a powerful and destructive force that you should attempt to avoid at all costs. It is closely tied to fear, which, we have previously established, will freeze you in your tracks. You are both imperfect; all of us are. Our salvation journey is the point. God does not need us to do anything; with a blink of His eye, everything He desires can be accomplished. Your mission is primarily for your benefit, in the sense that He is molding you into the image of His Son. The only way you lose is to give up hope.

At the end of First Corinthians, chapter 13, verse 13, Paul writes, "And now these three remain: faith, hope and love. But the greatest of these is love." There is no doubt that Paul was correct in saying that love is the greatest of these; however, when hope is damaged, the bridge between faith and love is broken. Since hope is the most fragile and easily damaged, it makes sense that the demonic attacks would focus on destroying it.

God is faithful! When God promised Abraham a son, Sarah laughed, seeing only the decay in her ninety-year-old body. In response, God asked this question: "Is anything too hard for the Lord?" Of course not, yet we struggle daily with aspects of our lives which are His to control. Submission and obedience are at the very heart of faith, hope, and love. They are how we find His peace in the middle of third world chaos and tragedy. Thankfully, He is patient with us and provides constant reminders that He is ultimately in control.

Lesson 8: Hope Is the Bridge

Jehovah-Rophe (The Lord Heals)

Lord, surely You Yourself have borne my grief and carried my sorrows. You were pierced through for my transgressions and crushed for my iniquities; the chastening for my well-being was upon You, and by Your scourging I am healed. You Yourself bore my sins in Your body on the cross, that I might die to sin and live to righteousness (Isaiah 53:4–5; 1 Peter 2:24).

Crushed, broken, emotionally, physically, and spiritually exhausted, I returned from the July 2012 trip. Unspeakable anger toward God consumed me, along with utter hopelessness for the lost people of the Mountain of Death. Maybe someday I will be smart enough to think before I ask for something. Before the July trip I had asked God to show me the bad, the hurting, and the lost; surely He answered my request. Slowly and patiently, God dealt with me, convicting me concerning our newest mission.

This trip was orchestrated by someone else and arranged in the inverse order from my July trip. The first two days would be spent at our compound. The first task was one dear to my heart, meeting with the founders to discuss the possibility of keeping the compound as our primary guesthouse in Haiti. The result of the meeting was that we would still use our former compound as one of our guesthouses for future team trips. I was extremely pleased with this result, as I had assumed a long distance parental feeling and responsibility for many of the children there.

As night began to fall, no supper was in sight, and my blood sugar was crashing. I was hoping that they had not forgotten me. I was such an American, thinking about myself and not the fact that no one else had eaten either. Soon afterward, I was asked to sit at the private table in the founder's quarters. Legume (Haitian stew), which is one of my favorite meals, was prepared for me. I was told that the adults were still away, and two of my favorite children would be joining me for dinner. This is an uncommon practice, as the adults and children are normally fed separately. Being Sicilian, I have grown up in a culture that fosters family dinners where much of the sharing and learning take place. We had a wonderful dinner and made lasting memories. The next day went way too fast, filled with teacher seminars, beach with the kids, and an evening filled with games and laughter.

The next day the Mississippi team arrived about noon. As we were loading up, my brand-new hiking boots were stolen while we were standing right there; although I was oblivious, this was an omen of things to come. Just as we were about to leave, a mother carrying an obviously sick baby approached me. She explained that the baby (Lena) was HIV positive and that she no longer could properly care for her. The founder of our mission organization was part of this team heading for the mountains. He and I had previously discussed our different feelings concerning children in need. He said he would first consider how he would pay for a child's care before acting, and I said that I would take the child first and then figure how I would cover the cost. However, no matter what his mouth said, I knew his heart. I pointed at him and told her to take the baby to him. After a short discussion, he agreed to take responsibility for Lena. My sister and her family became Lena's sponsors for the next two years until we placed her in an American-run home for children with HIV.

Previously we had been in agreement not to bring first-time visitors to Haiti into the mountains, yet we had peace about bringing this team from Mississippi. I seldom hit it off right away with people, but God bound this team together quickly. An extremely long and dangerous ride seemed to go quickly as we spent much of the time in conversation. We arrived in Pestel late, rushed through a quick dinner, and hit the beds about midnight.

Just before 4:00 a.m., I felt something on my back inside my shirt that startled me. As I began to doze off, I felt something higher on my back; I jumped out of bed just as it exited my collar. I had visions of a tarantula, but as we shone the light, it turned out just to be a field mouse. As I tried to settle in again, the market began to fill with the day's vendors. Haitians are not quiet, and the noise quickly became excessive. Soon a woman dressed all in white appeared, screaming and praying in Creole; the only discernible word was *Hallelujah*. We believed that she was casting out demons, but our only interpreters slept through the whole event, and thus we will never know what she was really doing.

Soon after dawn we climbed into the same little dinghy with the same Haitian pilots, except this time it was a beautiful day, and the seas were calm and serene. It suddenly occurred to me that I had not experienced any fear on this trip; God must have changed something within me. The visit to Billard went extremely well, as we laid the foundation for a future partnership with the village pastor and elders. They blessed us with another incredible meal and more of their incredible cinnamon flavored coffee. The children all looked very nice, dressed in their Sunday best for us. The pastor's son was married to a very nice Haitian woman who had complete control of the children. If she even looked at the children, their behavior changed immediately. She was also the children's Sunday school teacher, and it was obvious who was in charge. As we climbed down, she joined us. A comment was made to the pastor's son that he was a lucky man. I had never seen a Haitian turn as red as she did.

The next day we wound our way over the red clay goat path, dodging boulders and squeezing past trees as we approached the worst village on the mountain, Cayes LaSalle. The constant nightmares I'd had since my last visit had made me dread this moment and drained me of all enthusiasm about this trip. We were immediately inundated with villagers who were straining to see what we'd brought them. It was obvious the Mississippi team had come to work: they quickly unloaded the rice, beans, and underwear we had brought.

I was suddenly and amazingly free to do what I wanted. I began snapping pictures of the children, which is not a surprising activity for me. The Holy Spirit quickened me, and I showed the first girl her picture. All of a sudden, something amazing happened; she smiled. When I had visited the previous July, all the children had hopelessness in their eyes and were all at different stages in the death process; some were starving, some were loaded with parasites, and still others were diseased. Picture after picture, the children were smiling; then the laughing and giggling began. Praise God, the healing had begun! As it turned out, two weeks after we left in July, a team of doctors had arrived. It is amazing what a twenty-five-cent worm pill and some rice and beans will do for a child.

The children were soon organized into lines of boys and girls. The

Mississippi pastor ran the boys' line and his wife the girls' line, while a member of their church strummed softly on his guitar. On first look, underwear seemed like a trivial, silly gift, but this could not have been further from the truth. There, deep within the "Mountain of Death," a multitude of diseases and parasites waited to invade an unsuspecting host. The underwear covered and protected a main access point and thus protected the children. The children were incredibly happy with the gifts. You would have thought we were handing the girls Gucci dresses and the boys Armani suits. It was then that it occurred to me that these children had never held anything brand-new.

There was still no sign of my little angel Josie, and my anxiety was peaking as one of our staff showed the villagers her picture. Finally, one of the men said that she was coming. Shortly the little angel appeared, and she looked so good. Her bloated belly was gone, and she was now worm-free. Her personality was emerging in her tiny three-year-old frame as she made funny faces every time I took a picture of her. I was smiling as we drove away, realizing that God's healing of this village had actually healed me as well. I had a myriad of reasons to continue working in Haiti, but if I only had my little mountain angel as a reason, I would have still made the arduous and harrowing journey as often as God allowed me.

The night ended with a pleasant dinner and a great night's sleep at the pastor's house. The morning service was incredible. As the Mississippi pastor knelt to wash our host pastor's feet, the Holy Spirit fell. It was amazing to see the pastor melt in God's presence and equally refreshing to be refilled by the Holy Spirit personally. Tired but refreshed by God, we climbed back into the truck for a full day's ride back to Port-au-Prince. As we approached the River Glace, it became obvious that the waters had risen. The previous week a tap tap bus had been washed away, killing sixty people. Before we had a chance to discuss the situation, the driver stepped on the gas. The truck began to be carried away by the river. I have never prayed in tongues so quickly, as I then felt what I believe to be an angel or two push the truck back onto the river covered road. God had broken me the past July because I had asked Him to. Angry and indignant, I had lashed out at Him upon my return. During this trip, He healed me simply because He loves me in all my imperfect ways.

As you can clearly see, though I was damaged and somewhat out of control, God was not. He knew what I needed to learn, and when the opportune time arose, He demonstrated His great mercy by healing me. He will do the same for you. I pray that this helps readjust your perspective while God is healing your heart.

In His love,

Pastor D

My Dearest Macy and Mark,

I would like to take a moment and discuss the fruit of the Spirit found in Galatians chapter 5. Modern Protestant versions list nine fruits of the Holy Spirit, while the Latin Vulgate lists twelve. I would propose that combining the two would lead to thirteen fruit. The Protestant versions begin with love, which is undeniably the first fruit. The Vulgate includes charity, modesty, and chastity and differentiates longanimity (forbearance) from faith. The Protestant version of the list makes the assumption that the nine fruits listed cover all twelve of the Vulgate fruits. My purpose is not of a theological origin; rather, no matter which list of fruit you use, the fruits are obviously ordered for purpose. What I mean is that one flows from the other in a downhill progression.

I find it obvious that love is listed first, but intriguing that joy is listed second on both lists. In my own life, I can attest to the fact that if I do not have joy, then I also do not have peace. Once that downhill progression is broken, I may still have love, but the rest of the fruits deteriorate quickly. Joy is not trivial and should never be viewed in a supercilious manner. Keeping our joy under adverse conditions is paramount to our success and connection to the Holy Spirit. I have not always been able to maintain joy; it is one area where others assist me as I rax from the slumber of self-indulgent trauma.

Lesson 9: Joy, the Elusive Fruit

The Phoenix

Traditionally, in the legend of the phoenix, there is only one phoenix at a time, and it lives for a very long time. When it is near death, it builds a pyre and sprinkles aromatic herbs over it and then consumes itself in flames. Out of the ashes of this fire, a new phoenix arises. The phoenix places the ashes in an egg and carries it to Heliopolis, the city of the sun in Egypt. Because of its life cycle, the phoenix is also a symbol of rebirth. I felt very strongly about this name but somewhat troubled because of its ties to mythology and the ancient world. Recently, I have been at peace with the name because of the symbolism associated with it. This whole trip was about the old dying and the new being birthed.

As our journey unfolded, the obvious struck me. God was changing my heart concerning our previous compound to make space for our new guesthouse in Gressier. As I meditated during the trip, I realized this change was much more than a physical locale; rather, new leaders were being birthed, and a glimpse of the future in God's wonderful adventure was being revealed. Every trip is accompanied by a pretrip attack, sometimes subtle and sometimes not. We all go through this process, although the inexperienced may not recognize its occurrence. I tend to become despondent and even angry with myself at my inability to conquer my own foibles. The Holy Spirit reminds me that I am incapable of conquering anything on my own and that changes occur through Him and by Him. I do not really care for that answer, but obedience is a prerequisite for God's service.

I was also quite disconcerted about not traveling to the mountains to check on Josie and the other children. I wondered how I would react to going back to flatland ministry when I knew of the extraordinary need in the mountains. The answer was simpler than I had imagined: God created me to teach and disciple, which creates great joy within me. Watching this team grow in the Lord before my own eyes was more than I needed.

Pastor M and I take our responsibility to our teams extremely seriously. No matter your age we treat you like our children when you serve with us—not in a condescending manner but rather in a protective and loving manner. We must exude this feeling, because the team quickly began calling us their parents in Haiti. Perhaps because of our age difference or perhaps because of the love of God, the team did feel like family and the girls like daughters.

Pastor M has a servant's heart and continuously thinks of the needs of others before her own. Her maternal instincts are very strong, and it is easy for people to see her as a maternal figure. She worked quietly and tirelessly all week to make sure that everyone was taken care of, nothing glamorous but oh so important. I can honestly say that next to the Holy Spirit she was the reason that this trip was so joyous. Whether cleaning Kefira's knee, checking on Sarah when she was sick, setting up the medical bags, or cooking and cleaning for the team, she made it happen. She instinctively knew that this trip was all about the growth and experience of those whom we now call our three little white Haitian daughters. Karen and Sarah were chosen to lead what looked like a team composed of an additional ten teenagers. Slowly but methodically the teens dropped from the trip until Kefira stood alone. At times this process depressed me as I struggled with what I thought should be a teen trip. God is so great! The sense of joy, love, family, and trust were immediate on this trip, simply because not I but God had chosen the people.

Anxiety permeated the air as the team waited impatiently to depart. Our flight was delayed more than four hours, and the enemy used this the time to instill doubt concerning the mission in the team's minds. Once in PaP, we bypassed the usual city tours and headed straight for my favorite orphanage. The pastor who runs this orphanage is atypical in the sense that he considers all sixty-six orphans his own children. This is an abnormal mindset in Haiti; most orphanages run on the business model, making the orphans commodities by which to raise money.

We had planned a barbecue for the orphans, but we were far too late; thus, after a quick tour we left the supplies, promising that we would return the following Sunday. We needed to meet with the real estate broker to pay for the lease on our new mission house in Gressier. After a too-lengthy meeting with the Realtor, we were able to tour the new mission house, which was large and full of potential but also filthy and musty. I was worried about bringing the team to stay here on our last two nights in Haiti. We finally arrived at our former compound just before dinner, exhausted but relieved that we had finally reached our destination. As I looked around at the faces composing our team, the Holy Spirit revealed something I had not yet surmised. Outwardly, our team looked extremely weak, a team that would crumble and cry at the first sign of trouble, running home with their tails between their legs like a beaten Haitian dog. The truth was entirely different; this team had something that would terrify the enemy all week. They were all here because of a sincere desire to serve the Lord, endowed with love, joy, and peace concerning this mission that they had undertaken. Whenever obstacles would arise, this team would turn to the Lord in prayer, and our faithful God answered on each occasion.

During the week, we went door to door on four separate outreaches, praying for people's needs and distributing food. Each of these outreaches was a huge blessing and turned out to be one of the strengths of this team. Our first stop was Locul, where Pastor M and I prayed at the first two houses. Karen prayed at the third home, and that was all she needed as she then jumped at every opportunity to pray for people. Sarah followed suit; as the anointing fell upon her, she gained confidence, and you could actually see the Lord working in her and through her, changing this shy girl into a mighty prayer warrior. Kefira hung back for a while until I asked her if she was ready. She hesitated for a moment until it looked like Karen would jump in; she spoke up and said that she would pray for this man. From that point on, the rotation of prayer was seamless for the rest of the week.

During the course of the week, many extremely impoverished people simply asked us to pray for more of God and His blessings upon their family. It was humbling to watch their joyful desire for simply receiving more of God. Many people received Jesus as their savior, and countless healings took place as we prayed. We came up against several voodoo-held households, yet the team remained unscathed because of God's love.

We came upon a blind man's home during our last day of prayer. He simply asked for more of God; however, as we discovered later, several of us heard from the Holy Spirit to pray for his sight. The enemy won this battle as he convinced us that we were not really hearing from God. We were all sad when we learned that we had not fulfilled God's command; however, He is faithful to redeem and brought the man to the next day's clinic so we could pray for his eyes. He never regained his sight as far as I know, but God touched his heart, and he later took in his three granddaughters, who blessed our hearts dearly as we developed our ministry on the hill. Every day when we drove back and forth to feed the malnourished twins, Piper, Prudence, and their younger sister, Phoebe, would run to the edge of the property and smile and wave, waiting to hear us yell, *"Nou renmen ou"* (We love you). Being able to obey God and pray for this man's eyes brought the team great joy and alleviated our pain and the sense of guilt that we were feeling concerning our disobedience.

This was a small yet powerful team. During the week's clinics and feedings, the team performed as if they had been serving together for years. Kefira was my newest and youngest teen leader back in the States. Watching their growth during our outreaches brought me great joy. We all laughed, joked, and demonstrated the love of Christ through our every action and gesture. I could not have been prouder of them. As we headed to Gressier and our new mission home, I felt as though the trip was winding down; thankfully, God had saved the best part of the trip for last.

Once we arrived at our new mission home, we were unpleasantly surprised by the home's unfinished state. The painters were still working, and the floor was so dirty that the color of the tiles could not be perceived. We had neither electricity nor water, and the bathrooms were just nasty, with used prophylactics littering the bottom of each dry toilet. My first thought was to take the team to the American compound in PaP; Pastor M's first thought was to get to work cleaning our new mission home. She worked nonstop for the next six hours, and the whole team pitched in to help. By bedtime we had consumed a great meal and had clean floors and beds and one clean bathroom. The only running water was from an outside hose that the girls took into the servants' bathroom so they could shower. Hearing their comments and squeals from the icy cold water brought me more laughter than I could remember. It was a memorable evening full of laughter and love.

Our final day began with service at my favorite orphanage; translated, its name means "Home for the Poorest Children." I introduced the team and offered the invocation. This was followed by Kefira's inspirational message to the orphan children about success. Women in Haiti, as in much of the third world, are not afforded the same opportunities as men and are at constant risk of both physical and sexual abuse. Thus, seeing this pretty, exuberant sixteen-year-old speaking about success was highly motivational for the scores of young girls listening.

Sarah then led worship, which created an atmosphere of praise and love that enveloped the audience. Karen finished the service with a powerful first message on King David and overcoming giants. The children at this orphanage were mostly young and very cute. Valentina and Moses really touched me deeply. Moses received his name from the pastor because he was rescued from the water just as his namesake was. He exudes coolness in attitude as he dances or struts in his shades. Two little sisters also touched my heart as we learned they'd been abandoned in a banana field. Terrified, they just curled up for three days until they were found and rescued.

It was brought to our attention that the orphanage could not pay their rent and that they soon would be homeless. I spoke with Kefira privately, and she immediately agreed that we would help them. Once back in the States, she spearheaded the drive and raised a year's rent for the orphanage in less than three weeks. Each day she would come to my classroom and take the donation bucket to the lunchroom. She was well known, liked, and respected by the students, and she could get away with saying things like "I know how much that hamburger cost; please donate your change." This sixteen-year-old raised three thousand dollars in three weeks through spare change. God was beginning to use her in mighty ways.

After dedicating our new mission home, we held the last team meeting on the roof. The majesty of God shone through the star-filled sky as we all shared our joys and our pains. It was a special night and a special week as each of these three young women demonstrated their kingdom leadership potential.

On the way home, we were separated going through customs. As Kefira was the only minor, I kept her with me, and Karen and Sarah stayed together. Our line moved much faster than theirs did, and we were pulled out so Kefira could be questioned. Apparently, when they saw that we were not related, they thought I might have kidnapped her. She was quite flustered; however, I kept my sense of humor, realizing that eventually they would figure out that it was absurd to think that I kidnapped the little blond white girl from Haiti. We all breathed a sigh of relief but were still laughing as we exited the terminal. As I begrudgingly assimilate back into the first world, I will always cherish the time spent with our three little white Haitian daughters.

May God always give us His joy as we serve those who need us most! Macy and Mark, finding joy in the midst of serving on the front line is paramount to your success. Tears will come, and blood will flow; through it all, remember that the joy of the Lord is your strength.

In His love,
Pastor D

My Dearest Macy and Mark,

I would like to broach a subject where your expertise far outweighs my own. Although I am versed in both science and mathematics, I am a virtual novice when we are dealing with musical knowledge. There is a relevant connection between these three disciplines, which is beyond my current grasp. I believe that they are actually parts of a whole that leads us to a greater knowledge of who God is and how His power is made manifest. No matter how I am feeling, if I sing praises to Him from my heart, I feel better. It is not solely for our benefit though; His power flows through us when we become empty conduits.

There is a melody of harmonious music that we can faintly perceive when God's power flows. It is difficult to explain, yet definitely present. Each of us who serve on the front lines must find our way of tapping into that power through our submission and obedience to the direction of the Holy Spirit.

When I first noticed the correlation between God's power and music, I was intrigued and determined to examine what the correlation entailed. I vastly prefer the female voice, which led me to believe that the ability to hit the high notes like those of Mariah Carey was where the answer lay. I liked this premise because I take pride in the fact that God has given me the ability to rise to very high levels of performance for short times. After listening to Mariah's high notes, those sung in whistle tone, I realized that those notes were not pleasing to me and certainly not sustainable.

Next, I thought that the answer might lie within a singer's octave range. One of our favorite singers from our youth was Freddie Mercury, who boasted a highly acclaimed six-octave range; however, I still felt something was still not quite correct. Then the Holy Spirit had me reflect on who it was that I could listen to consistently without tiring of their voice. These were the same three women I listened to while weightlifting simply because their voices caused my adrenaline to surge, allowing me to sustain work at a higher intensity. I began to compare similarities between their voices. I found that all their voices were distinct and quite different from one another, but they shared a couple of similarities. For one, they were all classified as mezzo-sopranos. I was on the right track now as I finally realized that it was the way they were capable of maintaining resonant timbre while belting out powerful and sustained notes.

The lesson immediately became clear. It was not the head notes that appealed to me; rather, it was the powerful notes sung while belting in one's normal voice range. Belting is a specific technique of singing by which a singer mixes, in the proper proportions, their lower and upper registers, resulting in a sound that resembles screaming but is actually a controlled, sustained phonation. It was then that I realized that God had already taught me this lesson on one of our mission trips. I initially felt this mission to be a malicious conundrum, filled with dark sorrow and emotional trauma. It was not until later reflection that I began to fathom what God had done.

Lesson 10: Belt with God's Power

Maelstrom

The pretrip attack was more deceptive than normal, appearing as a series of incredible blessings followed by intense attacks. Lost and focusing solely on this roller coaster of highs and lows, I failed to perceive the chronic fatigue settling upon me. A maelstrom usually refers to a violent and powerful whirlpool; however, in this case, it refers to a restless, disordered, and tumultuous state of affairs.

Our team is small once again, composed of my primary leader Kefira and Lana, a leader in training. Our first night is difficult for Lana. She wonders why she came and has a burning desire to leave Haiti. We talk for a while as I convince her that this trip was not a mistake and that God will surely use her. This placates her temporarily, and she is able to fall asleep fairly quickly. The next day we are off to visit my favorite orphanage and my favorite little orphan, Valentina. When we arrive, Lana is not responding to the children; in fact she tells me that she does not really like children. I pray silently for her as Kefira and I engage the orphans.

There is something special about orphan children. They are acutely aware when someone is not all right—perhaps because that state is so familiar to them. Soon Moses, exuding his amazing swag, seeks her out. Shortly, he is donning her hat and sunglasses; hesitantly, she cautiously picks him up and holds him close. A smile slowly grows on her face until it's as wide as can be. God knew that she would find a special child and her purpose here among these orphans.

As we prepare to depart, my little orphan girl Valentina wraps herself around my leg so that I will not be able to leave her. Her simple gesture touches me deeply and profoundly. It's a moment in time that will be permanently and vividly ingrained in my memory.

The rest of the trip will be spent primarily holding mountain clinics. My young leaders pull me aside and request that I rename some of the terminology I use to define where we are. I have a great deal of respect for my young leaders, since they are all so pure of heart. When they advise me, I always take their advice into prayer. They have requested that the "Mountain of Death" be renamed the "Mountain of Hope." They have also coined the terms the "Magic Kingdom" and the "Tragic Kingdom" to replace the terms *first world* and *third world*.

As the mountains loom on the horizon, I wonder how I will endure another ten hours over the roughest terrain I have ever traversed. I am literally willing my body to move and overcome the total exhaustion encompassing my being. The drive turns out to be a pleasant surprise as they have repaired the road all the way to the River Glace. As the truck ascends into the heart of the mountains, the Holy Spirit quickens me to stop where we had previously offered a woman food and prayer for her many children. Much to my chagrin, we find her house gone and a parking area for the heavy road machinery in its place. I am momentarily perplexed as to why the Holy Spirit would have us stop here.

Before long, dirty, emaciated children appear from the mountain jungle, barely dressed in rags. Many are obviously sick as we form a circle among our small team and pray for guidance for us and mercy and provision for these little ones. We hold a miniclinic for the thirty or so children and give each a small bag of rice and beans to bring home. As we arrive at our mountain base camp in Jolie Gilbert, the air has become crisp and clear; this will be our most restful night's sleep.

I am up before dawn, praying that the delicious Haitian coffee will be ready soon, when I hear faint music in the distance. As the music gets louder, I get to the road just in time to witness my first voodoo parade. I am not afraid—only mesmerized as if I were watching an exciting documentary on television. Later that day we begin our clinic ministry in the mountain villages.

It was said that I would prophesy on this trip. I had been polite, but I was thinking that this pastor really should stop smoking crack. While we were visiting Cayes LaSalle where my little mountain angel Josie lives, we decided to pray. A Haitian pastor had joined us, one we'd had dubious and shady dealings with in the past. As we held hands, I began to pray, and my prayer turned into prophecy. I was in shock; I could not have stopped speaking if I had tried. As the prophecy came forth, the pastor's head shot up, and when our eyes met, I could see the evil within him. Although he did not understand a word of English, he knew exactly what the prophecy meant. The climax of the prophecy stated that when the people of Cayes LaSalle bent their knees to Jesus, then the whole mountain would fall under His will.

This was the last time we visited this village, as a silly little ministry turf war broke out over who would serve each village. The fact that ministries wanted credit for what they were doing hurt me tremendously and left a very bad taste in my mouth; silly me, I thought it was about bringing the good news of the gospel to the hurting and lost. Have our greed and avarice so consumed us that we will not reach out to save a dying child? In effect, the enemy had stopped me from helping the prophecy come to pass. However, God does not need me in order to accomplish His will.

The next day we visited Malkushan for a village feeding and introduction of our ministry to the village. On our way, we passed through another village that was having market day. They had made tarp canopies to protect themselves from the sun. This forced us to place some of our Haitian staff on top to the vehicle so they could move the tarps and allow our vehicle to pass. Between the crowds of people and the tarps, it took forty-five minutes to drive the mile through the village. Needless to say, Lana and Kefira were feeling anxious as we inched our way through.

It had become brutally hot by the time we arrived. The pastor told us their water was a problem and asked us to walk to see their water supply while the food was being prepared. It was a long walk, only to arrive at what I would call a swamp. Although it was fed by an underground spring, the water was stagnant and foul smelling. This was the same water source for both Cayes LaSalle and Cafayier. On the way back, Lana began to feel ill. I did not want to feed her in front of starving children; thus, we hid her in the vehicle and had her eat a peanut butter and jelly sandwich and rehydrate herself.

Once she felt better, we were able to assess the children while they ate. Their condition was much like it was on my first visit to Cayes LaSalle. One little girl was completely blond. She was wearing a long sleeve sweater and long pants. I rolled up her sleeves and pulled up her pant leg to reveal that her extremities were simply bones covered by skin while her stomach was hard and distended. I felt a sickening feeling welling up from deep in the pit of my stomach at this haunting sight. We had been given expensive village water treatment filters and agreed that they should have one. This never actually occurred because another ministry brought them house-sized filters shortly after our visit, which further exacerbated the tension between ministries. I never did return to Malkushan.

What should have felt like a mission of joy and accomplishment turned out to feel more like a bloodbath in my spirit. Perhaps I had become a little apathetic and satisfied with our meager accomplishments. God needed to shock me and remind me of the plight of the hurting and dying children strewn across this country. Luke 12:48 says, "From everyone who has been given much, much more will be demanded, and from the one who has been entrusted with much, much more will be asked." Perhaps this week was God simply asking for more. With all this said, there are still children under our influence who are at great risk. Through the many accomplishments, laughter, and tears shed this week, I realize that our shared experiences brought us much closer together as we carried out God's plan. For us to be able to sustainably belt with God's power, we must come to understand the most important factor: His power is best demonstrated through our weakness.

In His love,
Pastor D

My Dearest Macy and Mark,

I know you both will agree with me that God is omniscient. I expect you will also agree with me that we are not. Even though we know this, we need to be reminded of this continuously in the field. We do not need to always know the plan, only obediently walk it out. Many times I thought I was going to minister in a certain way, only to discover that God wanted me to do something completely different. I cannot stress enough the need for flexibility and adaptability in the field. The following is an account of one mission trip where we were absolutely clueless, and we just simply followed God.

Lesson 11: We Serve an Omniscient God

An Enigmatic Journey

Deluged by a plethora of annoyances, unrested, unprayed, and unprepared, we board our flight to the Tragic Kingdom. Our itinerary is once again very full, but with a notable twist: there is no team per se to lead. Pastor M and I will be joining three pastors who are already on the ground. Feeling a little like excess baggage, I ponder why we are even going on this trip. I focus on the fact that this will be Pastor M's first trip to the mountains, and if nothing else the venture will not be for naught.

My mood and demeanor quickly change as we are warmly greeted and learn we will be holding a clinic and hot dog outreach today. Everything runs smoothly as we are being filmed for the first time. This, however, will be my last moment in a comfort zone during this mission. We arrive at the new school later that day, where I am introduced as the new superintendent of the school. The previous day was a holiday; thus, only 30 percent of the children were present. This is a common occurrence in Haiti, and I feel that one of my priorities should be to actually create a school calendar.

The teachers are all cordial if not friendly and most likely wondering if I will muck up their system. Several significant events take place during this meeting. Our vehicle overheats and needs to be switched out, but more significantly, as I speak to the Haitian pastor about my ideas, I ask him his opinion. His answer both shocks and encourages me when he says that it doesn't matter what anyone thinks because God has brought me to help them and that they are in total submission to God's plan. I'm half expecting to be received as I was at our former compound school, where the teachers said yes to everything and did what they wanted once I left.

———◆✖◆———

The next event became a catalyst for change within my heart as the Holy Spirit began to show me His plan rather than my own. The father of two beautiful little girls had abandoned them after their mother had passed away. The church pastor had initially denied his request to care for the girls because he and his wife were old and destitute; however, his wife was full of faith that God would provide for the girls, which eventually changed his mind.

On three separate occasions, through three unrelated people, prophecy declared that I would be a general in God's army and that Pastor M would be the mother to thousands of children. As these humble servants of God took these little girls into their home, God confirmed His words to us. Some time later, two more sisters also needed to be taken, and the pastor and his wife also agreed to take them.

The drive to Pestel later that day was arduous and harrowing. The master cylinder was failing on one vehicle, which caused the brakes to be soft; the other vehicle's front seat was leaning back so far that it was impossible to get any back support while driving. Just before twilight, we pulled over for an impromptu barbecue. Once we resumed our trip, a box truck stuck in the mud delayed us for about two hours. Being trapped would have normally caused us a great deal of anxiety and a modicum of crankiness over such a diversion from our schedule, but the peace of the Lord settled on us as we patiently waited, basking in the glory of God's beautiful creation and great adventure.

We arrived at the guesthouse close to 11:00 p.m. and were immediately treated to a gourmet meal. Pastor M and I were given what I would consider Pestel's version of a honeymoon suite, with a king-size bed covered in beautiful linens and surrounded by mosquito netting. This room did not exist the last time I was here; it was almost as if God had prepared His very best for Pastor M so that she would feel at home and want to return.

The next morning we sailed to Billard for a medical clinic. We set up three stations: a dental check and toothbrush distribution; a worming evaluation with medical triage; and a shoe distribution. We had not wormed the children last July, and it was obvious by the abundance of Guinea worms, a sight that haunts me to this day. If I had double-checked the medical bag before the July trip, I would have noticed that the worm pills had been removed. When one is involved in discipleship, there must be a balance between trust and leadership during the delegation process. Ultimately, the leader is responsible for everything; this was an important lesson that I needed to learn in Haiti. The beautiful little five-year-olds' legs and arms now scarred by worms, because I did not check behind our team, is a haunting reminder of this lesson learned.

One of the Haitian voodoo traditions is to tie string around a baby's waist. The string is left in place until it breaks. The Haitians believe that once the string breaks, it means that the child will always be well fed. The result is many children with extended belly buttons. As I examined one little girl, I felt something under her shirt. I lifted her shirt and saw that what once was her herniated belly button was now hanging from a voodoo necklace around her neck. Before I could say anything, her mother grabbed the necklace, yanked it off, and threw it into the nearby brush.

All the help that Billard receives is through the pastor and his church. The fear of being exposed and subsequently ostracized was clearly written on this mother's panicked face. I could not believe she had mutilated her child; however, her fear calmed me somewhat, as I realized I was dealing with a cultural aspect that I did not fully understand. I wondered what I might have done if my own children were literally starving to death.

On our return, we detoured to a gorgeous deserted island to enjoy a relaxing swim in the warm aqua blue waters before heading deep within the mountain jungle to Cafayier. This was to be a new experience for us all and one we were not too comfortable with. We were going to spend the night in a traditional Haitian home. This was a humbling experience for us, as they gave us their very best, including sacrificing one of their cats for dinner. We faced a conundrum of conscience, as we have always had dogs and cats for pets. I vividly remember the pain felt when a beloved animal dies, which for me is usually accompanied with a myriad of tears. We spread our food out over the entire breadth of the plate and made sure that our hosts were not looking as we passed the plate of cat to other less sensitive members of the team when our hosts were not looking. The "*blan*" (whites) were then led to the master bedroom, while our staff was offered the rest of the beds, displacing our hosts and their children from their own home. I never learned whether they stayed with neighbors or slept outside on the ground.

We were four men along with my wife in the room. For safety's sake, a metal basin was placed in the center of the room in case we needed to urinate in the middle of the night. Of course the only one who needed to go was Pastor M. She waited until she thought everyone was asleep and slipped out of the mosquito netting and quietly made her way to the basin. As it was metal, the sound of her urination echoed in the room, and the other men were actually not asleep, as she had surmised. We all had a good laugh, which led to the story of how every time one pastor would get close to a certain donkey, it would react in a specific manner. I will leave it to your imagination as to how the laughter and subsequent dialog ensued. Needless to say, there was more laughing than sleeping that night.

The next morning we had planned an outreach at the village church; however, we popped a tire driving over the boulders, which delayed us for more than an hour. We decided to leave the clothing, shoes, and food for the pastor and instructed him to tell his people that those blessings were from Jesus. This was a powerful reminder to us all that as we struggle for brand recognition, we serve Jesus, and ultimately, without Him none of our ministry would ever take place.

We laughed and we loved many times over on this mission, but for me the greatest revelation was that God's plan for us was still an enigma. We did not have the vaguest clue concerning His plan for us. He said go, to which we replied yes, and that was the singular point. He wants our total trust and faith so that He may create our ultimate God adventure—one filled with Him and not our preconceived notions of what we are supposed to accomplish. May His will always be accomplished in our lives!

In His love,

Pastor D

My Dearest Macy and Mark,

I realize that I have spent an inordinate amount of time preparing you for the tragic in the hope that I may somehow lessen your heartaches. I have not shared much concerning the countless blessings and rewards of being allowed to serve His children. The witnessing of His power and miraculous touch are inexpressible moments of joy that cannot be stolen from you. The time afforded to you to just play, sit, hold children, give a hug, and simply love are what our greatest memories are composed of, and they are simply priceless. Store up your joys for the dark days of pain, sorrow, and regret. Mary's memories of Jesus's miraculous birth gave her the strength to endure His scourging and crucifixion. "But Mary treasured up all these things and pondered them in her heart" (Luke 2:19).

The most powerful and indelible quote I ever heard was spoken at the Promiseland Church in Austin, Texas: "Don't die with seeds in your pockets." Most of the time we plant seeds and move on before we see what God will do with them. God allowed me to plant, water, and watch Kefira and Sela grow and produce very good fruit. They were the only leaders to remain with me their whole four years of high school. I will not only be forever grateful that He allowed me to see their maturation, but also grateful for the trust it instilled in me that when I plant seeds, He will faithfully tend them until they produce abundant fruit.

Lesson 12: Store God's Blessings

First World Problems (FWP) in the Fourth World

Restlessness and impatience have invaded my being. The ardor that I once felt has been supplanted by aspersions, cynicism, and doubt. Our first-world problems seem so artificial and self-indulgent to me. "Oh no, I used my last Pandora skip for an hour, and this song is even worse than the last."

This represents my state of mind as the plane touches down with my two young leaders, Kefira and Sela. I am both excited and nervous for Sela. She is sensitive like Pastor M, and her first mission trip to Haiti was akin to a Girl Scout picnic compared to what we have planned for this mission. With other prospective members of the team having pulled out at the last moment, I am beginning to feel this trip is a reward for these two great young leaders' faithful four years of service. They have led together for the past two years, yet they have never had the opportunity to build the kind of relationship that is deep and intimate like those formed on a mission trip.

Upon clearing immigration, we make excellent time to our first orphanage. We spot my favorite little orphan girl, Valentina, almost immediately, but she does not respond to our arrival. I ask the pastor if she is sick; he replies no and calls her over. She allows us to hold her, but she is not acting like the smiling, affectionate baby she has been in the past. I am still quite concerned about her as the hot dogs are now ready to serve. My two leaders jump into action, and the children are fed in record time. We have no time to play on this trip; even I think that I may have overscheduled our itinerary. I am unsure what we are capable of accomplishing; thus, I push a little harder on each mission trip. Our time comes to an end too quickly as we speed off to our guesthouse in Gressier. As we pull away, my mood is sullen as I continue to worry about Valentina. The remainder of the day is spent in preparation for our mountain mission, packing food bags for door-to-door evangelism, and preparing the medical supplies for the mountain clinics. The Wi-Fi is not working properly, and I struggle with it until I learn that the network is being repaired. Later that evening, I am finally able to get a message out that we have arrived safely.

As day two begins, the Wi-Fi is still not working and I find myself beginning to get angry. Sela has never been to the mountains and is feeling some anxiety, which increases mine as well. I am normally acutely aware of the omnipresent physical and spiritual dangers when we make this trek, but as we begin our long ride, I am oblivious to the fact that I am under a spiritual attack. As we travel, Kefira and I have difficulty staying awake, even though my head is continuously bounced against the headrest. The enemy comes to me in my comatose state and whispers that he is going to kill me—to which I reply that I may be injured while serving God only if He allows it. I tell Jesus that if He wants me to come home, I am ready. This is a very unusual posture for me because of my concern for the five billion plus unsaved souls on the planet. A more normal response from me would be to pray for more time, money, and workers to reach the hurting and unsaved.

We arrive safely at our base camp in Jolie Gilbert with several hours of daylight still left. This is a welcome surprise, as arriving in the dark may add to the uneasiness of the treacherous journey here; however, the light coupled with freedom from the confines of the truck have brought smiles to my young leaders' faces as expectancy builds towards the coming day's mission.

We awake to a beautiful morning on the mountain after a crisp, restful night's sleep. I thought I'd been clever to schedule our boat departure on an off market day in Pestel. Much to my chagrin, New Year's Eve is one of the largest market days of the year in Pestel. We keep a tight line as we push through the mass of flesh toward the dock. Although we are an hour late, the boat is still not ready for us. I finally breathe a sigh of relief as we push away from the dock on our way to Billard.

Once we dock, Kefira sprints ahead with the children, leaving Sela and me huffing and puffing as we make the arduous climb toward Billard. I am acutely aware of my lack of physical readiness and vow to return in better condition for the summer's mission. I grow concerned for Sela, as she is struggling both physically and mentally. The enemy is attempting to crack her, but God has other plans for her today.

Once we arrive at Billard, we quickly organize the clinic as God quickens me to a unique plan for such a small team. The plan should have never worked, yet under the direction of the Holy Spirit the clinic begins smoothly. As I triage the children, I call out direction for my leaders who are treating each child. Only Kefira has experience treating children in our clinics, yet they work seamlessly together.

About five minutes into the clinic, Sela becomes ill from the enemy's final attempt to break her. We sit her down and give her water and gummy candies for sugar. Within another five minutes, she is feeling better and wants to rejoin the clinic. I suggest she should rest a little longer, but she replies, "I'm fine. I didn't come to Haiti to sit." The Holy Spirit quickens me to the fact that the former Girl Scout is now a mighty warrior in God's army.

Once the clinic ends, we are led to the village center and treated to a delicious meal consisting of tubers and conch with plenty of Billard's famous cinnamon coffee. The younger pastor's wife gives me a Pastor M type hug, which completely catches me off guard, while the lead pastor's wife hands me a pound of their exquisite coffee for Pastor M. These simple gestures confirm to me that we are becoming part of the Billard family.

As day three begins, we are scheduled to feed the children of Cafayier; however, because of the drought, the women of the village must search for water, and the feeding has been delayed until three. I ask why we did not provide the water, and the answer was that no one thought of it. Left with a large opening in our itinerary, I search my heart and ask the local pastor if there is a new village that needs our help. The pastor confirms that there are indeed very needy villages not receiving any aid. Although apprehensive about taking my young leaders, I decide that the Holy Spirit will lead us and not give us more than we can handle.

We hike at a brisk Haitian pace for forty-five minutes into the mountain jungle and arrive at a small rickety church located in the village center of LeFevre. The local pastor disappears into the jungle for about an hour as a few children begin to appear. They look pretty good; they have decent clothes and are moderately well dressed. Kefira and Sela look at me as if to say, *We hiked all this way for this.* We are bored and hot as I decide that we will worm and treat the few children standing with us.

As we begin, other children appear, and the condition of each new group of children is worse than the last. Their tattered clothes now adorn dirty, malnourished children. The local pastor finally arrives and greets us warmly and sincerely. As we speak, he tells me that if we plan a summer clinic, a thousand children might come. We agree to return for a large clinic and feeding for the summer and say our goodbyes.

As we begin our hike out of the jungle, a frantic man stops us. His baby is sick, and he wants us to look at her. The mother appears shortly and is suffering from extreme malnutrition that has stopped her milk production. The baby is about five months old and is also severely malnourished. Her little legs are only the size of my pinky finger, and she is not tracking well with her eyes. We lay our hands on the baby and pray for God's mercy and healing to be upon her. As I open my eyes, I see tears streaming down the faces of my young leaders. Before we leave, I give the pastor money for formula for the next two weeks, which he agrees to buy in Pestel later that day.

The village feeding at Cafayier goes well later that day. We are overjoyed to see that Josie's uncle has brought her over from Cayes LaSalle. This is quite unusual, since the villages have an ongoing rivalry over American aid. She is getting taller, and although still too thin, otherwise she looks well. It breaks my heart that she walks with the other village children the almost eight miles to school in Pestel. Cafayier is more unruly than usual, as the non-Christians have been on a three-day drinking binge celebrating the New Year. The feeding goes well; still, I remove us from the potentially dangerous scene the moment the last child is fed.

It is well past dark when we arrive back at our mountain base camp. I am a little sad as this is the first time in twenty-five years that Pastor M and I have not ushered in the New Year together. I realize that everyone is experiencing the same type of feelings. Our team is not blood related, but we are definitely family.

The next morning, none of us is ready to leave the mountains, which normally is a sad and depressing experience. On our way down, we stop to visit another new village, T-Plaine. This village also has a great need, and we decide to add them to our mountain clinic rotation. The road to

T-Plaine almost disappears toward the end, even passing through a large riverbed with a steep incline on the far side.

On one of our visits, their pastor really impressed me. As we were just beginning our clinic, it began to rain heavily. The pastor stopped us and said that we must leave so that the river did not block our departure. It is highly unusual for Haitians to care more about us than their own people. This simple gesture touched us deeply and caused us to become more committed to the village. On our way back we also tried something new. I had wrestled with the wisdom of my plan, and thanks to the Holy Spirit, it turned out to be the correct decision. On the way back to Gressier, we stopped at Locul and fed the children a late hot dog lunch that helped us transition back into flatland ministry seamlessly.

The following day we spend at our former compound, and there are new children everywhere. The feeling is light and welcoming, much as it was in the beginning. We have a wonderful day with the children and great stories from the founders. Kefira and Sela have both found their special child, Kefira's at Locul and Sela's here today. It is amazing how, from all the loving children, God selects one special child for each visiting team member. The bond that forms here is immediate and strong; in fact, when we later return without Sela, little Caroline bursts into tears.

The next day finds me reunited with my sweetheart, Pastor M. Although we have only been apart for a week, it feels more like a month. We begin a series of seven orphanage visits today. The conditions vary greatly between them, and we will visit the worst two today. Our first stop is the orphanage with ninety children in PaP. We bring enough food to feed the children for the next two weeks and stay just long enough to give everyone hugs and love. We spend the bulk of the day in Canaan with the "Flower Lady" at the tent city orphanage. My heart breaks for the children here, as she is running very low on supplies. They have food but no charcoal with which to cook it, and their medical cabinet is less stocked than mine is at home. I give her a few medical supplies and money for charcoal before we pray for the children. We won't quickly forget the tiny emaciated bodies of these little ones.

◆━◆※◆━◆

All too soon it was time for our last team meeting. Pastor M and Sela were the most emotional, fighting back tears because their time was up, and neither was ready to leave. Kefira was determined that she and I would make the most of our last two days. We began by holding an orphanage clinic for the orphanage that houses my favorite little orphan, Valentina. It was amazing to see my young leader work, literally by herself, as I triaged the children. We had brought them about a week's worth of food, as their supplies were also running low.

We spent the afternoon at the American compound in PaP, which had grown to care for one hundred and fifty children. We watched as they drained the fluid from the head of a baby who was suffering from encephalitis. Her body was frail and small, yet her head was swollen to the size of a soccer ball. Thankfully, I was alone when they turned her over, exposing her deformed face and soul-piercing soft brown eyes. She died shortly after we left, and I can still vividly picture this dying baby. Perhaps I am never supposed to forget her!

Our last day was our busiest, a blessing to distract our minds from our impending departure. Today belonged to Kefira. She single-handedly treated the whole village of Marose as I triaged patients. During this trip, she honed her uncanny ability to survey an environment and find the one child who needed her the most. The speed at which she was able to accomplish this boggled my mind and convinced me that I could take her anywhere in the world as an invaluable asset.

We spent the afternoon at Project Eden, feeding the children a hot dog lunch, visiting Be Like Brit orphanage and the Respire Haiti School. This was one of my favorite mission trips, and we came close to finding our limit. My two young leaders will graduate this coming May, a day that I am selfishly not looking forward to. I treasure this trip in my heart so that when things appear bleak, I can draw upon the memories of the laughter, service, and love, remembering the good we do in His name and for His glory!

In His love,

Pastor D

My Dearest Macy and Mark,

I would like to address how we perceive events and explore the differences between our perspectives and God's. Having the ability to step back from a situation and view it through our Savior's eyes is an invaluable skill that will serve you well in the field. My intent is not to lay out a sad, wrenching recitation of my sorrows; rather, it is to represent God's majesty in spite of our shortcomings.

Some of my greatest victories preceded some of my greatest failures. It was during these times that God most often spoke prophetically, helping me realize both that it is not about me and that it is all about me. Humility is not thinking less of yourself; it is thinking about yourself less. It is God's job to think about you and orchestrate your life to become like our Lord Jesus. Recall one of my favorite versus, Ephesians 2:10: "For we are God's handiwork [workmanship, masterpiece] created in Christ Jesus to do good works, which God prepared in advance for us to do." Please read the next paragraph and decide what you would do before you continue reading.

Lesson 13: See through the Eyes of Our Savior

Perspectives

This is perhaps the worst thunderstorm you have ever driven through. The sheets of rain blast the windshield of your BMW Z4 Roadster. Blinded by the flashes of lightning and jumpy from the booming thunder, you grip the steering wheel tighter and hunch forward, straining to see. A light above a bus stop appears faintly in the distance. As you slowly approach, you can make out three drenched and shivering figures. You recognize the first immediately; he is an old war buddy who carried your unconscious, broken body from behind enemy lines, saving your life. The second is an elderly woman in apparent cardiac arrest. She needs immediate medical attention, or she will die. Suddenly, God speaks to your heart and you realize that your perfect God-given mate is the third person. Your spirit cries out for her, but wait, the other woman is dying, and this friend saved your life. You are certain that the bus will arrive before your return. What should you do, since you only have one other seat? Please make your choice before you continue reading.

This is a classic problem that demonstrates how our perspectives influence our values and choices. I gave this problem to my high school students, and their answers follow. Sixty percent picked up their friend. Their reasoning was equally divided between loyalty to the friend and fear of the two strangers. Thirty-four percent chose to save the dying woman, while 5 percent chose their perfect God-given mate.

Only 1 percent of the students were able to think outside of the box. You hand the keys to your friend, assist the woman in cardiac arrest into the passenger seat, and then return to your God-given mate while your friend drives to the hospital with the dying woman. As a missionary, you must think this way. In fact, it would be better to throw the box away since God rarely fits His plans into one.

Around this time, I read an article that infuriated me. It was titled "The Problem with Little White Girls: Why I Stopped Being a Voluntourist." Soon God began to speak to me and to enlighten me that from the writer's perspective she was absolutely correct. Normally, short-term mission trips do not accomplish lasting life change. Many times, they take up the missionary's time and consume valuable resources. Our experience was somewhat abnormal, in that we paid for all our outreaches and typically engaged in activities that needed many hands, such as medical clinics, village feedings, and mass clothing distribution. The ultimate point of short-term mission trips is simply to allow God the opportunity to kindle a fire within the volunteers concerning mission work. I have gone on a number of different trips where the trip's mission was adjusted to the skill sets of the volunteers.

In the last analysis, missions are about the salvation of souls and their subsequent discipleship; however, I cannot find one instance in which Jesus did not meet the physical needs of the people He was ministering to. This is the reason we have run feeding programs, medical outreaches, and educational classes in both our short-term ministry as well as in permanent assignment. God created me to teach, and so my every action, gesture, and outreach is part of the discipleship process. I know other pastors who need discipleship to be more deliberate. I am highly choleric and possess many of the negative sanguine markers, which makes others believe that I have a melancholy personality. The motivation that drives each of us and our unique perspectives may be different; however, the end result is always to bring forth the kingdom of God.

The spring mission trip was not extraordinary except for the fact that God changed my perspective concerning my call. I was quickly becoming all about the outreaches and less present in each moment. Our time seemed so short on each trip that I wanted to accomplish as much as humanly possible. I had lost my joy, which is found in the simplicity of loving the children.

God used three little girls to remind me why He sent me to Haiti. Several months ago, a compound child had been removed from our former compound. Although the events necessitated immediate removal, the unforeseen consequence was that she was ripped away from all the people she knew and loved. I was overjoyed to see her, and we made time to love on her. I immediately noticed several scars resembling burns on her upper chest and legs. All we were told was that she needed to return for her own protection.

We also visited Lena, who was gravely sick. I feared that her little HIV-ravaged body could not sustain itself against her current condition. Her father had passed away from HIV two months previously, and her mother was also losing her fight with the disease as a large tumor was growing on her neck. I held Lena close to my chest as I pleaded the blood of Christ over her and interceded for her, drowning out her congested cries.

Later that day we had scheduled a feeding at Locul. The kids were particularly unruly at first, requiring all my effort just to maintain the line. Once the feeding began, calm was renewed, and the outreach went smoothly. One of my experienced team members, Karen, came and told me about a young girl in line whom I needed to see. I knew the expression "so beautiful that it takes your breath away," but I had never experienced it until this moment. She was the epitome of a perfect little Haitian girl—magazine-worthy if she had been born in the United States.

From my perspective, our compound child would live a happy life within the compound border, and Lena would succumb to HIV at a young age. What occurred was quite different. The compound child stayed for about six months until she discovered boys and became unmanageable. She was sent to live with her uncle and seldom returns to the compound. Lena was placed in an American-run children's home that specializes in pediatric AIDS patients. She is thriving and very happy in her new environment.

I never saw the little girl from Locul again. I suspect that she will live in her family's six-by-ten shanty, fighting to avoid disease and famine, until she herself marries, has children, and watches helplessly as the cycle of poverty repeats, but who knows? God's perspective is very different from my own. This is the real world outside of the Magic Kingdom—a world in which you and I are able to make a difference as we bring relief, love, comfort, and the knowledge of Jesus Christ to a dying world. I believe God has realigned my perspective with His so that I now see that those of us filled with His Spirit are able to effect change in the lives of the children we serve.

In His love,

Pastor D

My Dearest Macy and Mark,

I am so happy that you have safely returned to school from your summer mission and that you are immersed in your second year schedule. I commiserate and empathize with you concerning the emptiness and depression you are feeling. Let me assure you that what you are feeling is quite normal. We were created to serve God and each other; thus, when we return from a country that allowed us to constantly live in this manner, it is natural to experience an emotional letdown. Exacerbating these feelings are the natural tendencies of guilt associated with experiencing a world of extreme need and suffering and then returning to a country of opulence and self-indulgence. It is crucial for you to learn to guard your heart and to step away with the Holy Spirit so that He may heal and refill you, teaching you to process what you have experienced in a kingdom manner. It is a most difficult lesson, but one we must learn if we expect to serve Him full-time. "Toy Soldiers" is my recounting of a mission where my unguarded heart almost led to my destruction.

Lesson 14: Guard Your Heart

Toy Soldiers

> I have told you these things, that in me you may have
> peace. In this world, you will have trouble. But take heart!
> I have overcome the world. (John 16:33)

Everyone is more or less on time as we begin our journey. We clear security
fairly quickly, although the girls are stopped because of excess toiletries.
My youth leader, Kefira, is even subjected to a full body pat-down; she
willingly complies since they have agreed to let all her toiletries through.
This is her opportunity to lead in the third world; as I snap a quick
preboarding photo, God reassures me of her readiness.

We speed through customs in Port-au-Prince and are on our way to
our first ministry outreach at a very poor orphanage in less than half an
hour. I have overloaded our itinerary, necessitating an immediate start.
There are deeper reasons for this action as well. First-timers are sometimes
overwhelmed and shut down by the utter hopelessness, which seems an
inevitable part of the Port-au-Prince experience. This sometimes happens
quickly, before I am able to help them process what they are experiencing.
Instead, we try to place orphans in their arms as soon as possible so that
God has a chance to reveal why they came and help them understand that
they are not on vacation in any way, shape, or form.

We reach the orphanage before lunch and are greeted by a score of tiny
smiling faces. We first lead our team to the babies' room, the largest and
most comfortable room for teams. Kefira sets the example by snatching
up and cuddling with the first baby. The team then follows suit except
for Jenice; she is standing by the stairs with tears running silently down

her cheeks. I go to her and ask what is wrong, to which she replies, "It's all just so sad."

I explain that what she is experiencing is a necessity so she can grasp God's plan for her in Haiti. She reenters the room as I scan for unengaged children. One little girl is hiding between the bunk beds. I smile as I scoop her up and walk over to Jenice. Our eyes lock, and I ask, "Are you ready?" She reaches out as I place the toddler in her arms; they begin to cuddle almost immediately.

I now scan the room for Maya, my new leader. In my mind, the connection she makes to Haiti is crucially important. She will be my student advocate, Kefira's replacement, so to speak. She has found a young boy and is showering love upon him. Everyone is usually drawn to little girls because of their cuteness coupled with vulnerability; however, time and time again Maya will seek out the little boy who needs her most. Soon, a one-legged boy is entertaining us. He zooms around the room smiling and showing off for us. Although I must end his show abruptly, he demonstrates an important lesson to the team; poor, disabled, and hungry does not necessarily equate to miserable.

Once back at Gressier, we split into teams to prepare for the next couple of days' events. The next five days will be packed with numerous orphanage visits, feedings, door-to-door food distribution, and prayer, as well as several medical clinics. It will be a whirlwind of places, faces, and emotions. The team will be hot, cranky, tired, and hungry at times. Everything about their spoiled American nature will be challenged; yet when the week is finished, none will want to leave. This is the nature of Haiti, especially the trips I lead, where we serve sunup until sundown.

God is teaching and instructing me daily now. He is no longer satisfied with my narcoleptic periods of leadership or my itineraries carried out on autopilot. Except when my spiritual antennae are raised for danger in Haiti, I am rather a dullard when God is trying to make a point. For me ministry has always been about the accomplishment of tasks or the success of an event. I am event-driven by nature and capable of reaching great heights of performance for short periods. Perhaps it is the adrenaline rush of competition that I crave, coupled with my desire for change and healing in the children we serve.

Patiently, with mercy and grace, God is showing me that none of my previous assertions concerning Haiti is why He has me return time and time again. There will be no great Haitian reformation, no light bulb going off in Haitian minds. A hundred years from now no one will remember we existed or even went to Haiti.

So why do we risk our lives suffering for a hopeless cause? I know that I have asked that question on more than one occasion! The answer is neither difficult nor complex. We are living out Matthew 25:37–40 and Ephesians 2:10. We choose Haiti because we are not afraid. We know that when we are serving God, nothing can happen to us unless He allows it. As we live out the parable of the sheep and the goats found in Matthew 25, we teach and disciple our teams as well as the Haitians we partner with and minister to. Here lies the sweetest fruit of our work: watching God change our team, staff, and partners—and the children we love. It is the joy of watching God raise up Kefira and begin the process in Maya.

We must never forget what we are primarily called to do by the Great Commission. Therefore, the realization that Haitians are ingrained with ideas that insult or even hurt us is irrelevant. Bleeding the white man dry of all his money, time, and emotions may be taught. Saying yes and then doing whatever they want might be frustrating, and going to church in the morning and practicing voodoo in the afternoon may be ignorant. But it really does not matter. We must be obedient just as the apostles were. We carry out our mission, and if we are not received, then we shake the dust off ourselves and move on.

Our second day in Haiti was really interesting, as it was completely orchestrated by the Holy Spirit. We delivered food and prayed for people in the morning with a local pastor, fed the kids of Locul a hot dog lunch, and finished the day with more door-to-door food distribution and prayer during the late afternoon. The day was brutally hot but otherwise great. The team was overrun with Haitian children who desperately needed them, and they were also able to see firsthand what a real desire for God looks like.

Once again, as we asked for prayer needs, people living in abject poverty solely asked for more of God. Their humble nature and grateful spirits blew the team away. The faith of our team ran the entire gamut from spiritual warriors to prayer novices. By the end of the day, eight of the eleven-team members had laid hands on people and prayed for their needs.

Our third day was full of joy, laughs, and fun. We spent most of the day at Project Eden in Grand Goave. We played and loved on the children before serving them a hot dog lunch. Watching the team play Duck, Duck, Goose was a real treat for me. Abarrane has established herself as our official child magnet. Every place we go she is inundated with children. Many children could only lie silently in the shade, as the community was in the throes of a chikungunya outbreak, and many children were running high fevers. The severity of the children's infirmity prompted me to carry a medical bag with us from that day forward. We also promised to return the coming Saturday for an impromptu medical clinic before we left for the mountains.

I had been looking forward to the afternoon with both great expectation and trepidation. We were going to Petit-Goâve (Ti Gwav) to participate in prison ministry and fulfill the one area of the Parable of the Sheep and the Goats that I had yet to accomplish. My main fear was that my team was mostly composed of young females. We had the team dress ultra-conservatively before we plunged into our task. The behavior of the prisoners and the smells were not as bad as I had imagined; however, the living conditions in the men's prison were so abhorrent that we were made to leave our phones and cameras in the vehicles. Two cells approximately twenty feet by twenty housed one hundred and twenty prisoners on average. They were neither fed nor given water by the guards. The cells were festooned with raggedy, worn, torn, and foul-smelling hammocks, which seemed to hang from every square inch of the ceiling. The prisoners were at the mercy of the guards and the people who bring them food and water. Only about 20 percent of the prisoners, we learned, would ever stand before a judge. The others were released solely at the discretion of the guards who watch over them.

We fed the prisoners one cell at a time, splitting the team in two so that everyone would have the chance to serve. There were only a few catcalls but many more kissing sounds directed at our females. Most in our group said that it was not as bad as they had imagined, but I could tell from their facial expressions and mannerisms that the visit had left a lasting impression. Kefira, Maya, and I would return the next two Wednesdays to help feed the inmates. I do not believe that this ministry is part of my calling; however, I see great value in this ministry as well as certainly something that Jesus would have us do.

The following day was our first medical clinic in Marose and the first time for our new location. We had reclaimed a former voodoo temple and reconstructed it to house our clinics and discipleship training for the indigenous Christians. We set up a worming station and three treatment tables. Danya, our adult female chaperone, Kefira, and I would triage and give instruction to the rest of the team. This was now Kefira's fourth mission to Haiti and her first time triaging, as she had always been my primary assistant. She had done a wonderful job leading the team this week, and today was no exception. I enlisted Maya and Abarrane as my new assistants to ensure they were being trained. I believed they would be Kefira's replacements, each with an incredible heart for Haiti.

It was hot and crowded in the house with no clear pathways. It did provide separation from the massive crowds that sometimes became overwhelming for those new to clinics in Haiti. The team adjusted and learned quickly; seemingly adapting to every new case laid before us. The most severe case was a young girl with burns to her face, wrists, and hands. With the exception of Kefira, the rest of the team stood mortified as I treated her. I have come to learn that the buck stops with me on these missions. We dealt with how they were feeling at that evening's team meeting.

The afternoon was spent taking the compound children to the beach at Locul. Everyone had such a great time playing with the children on the beach and swimming. We took turns taking the youngest children into the water and making certain that none were left out. Joshua set himself up as the team comic relief. Whether it was running away from the naked little girl who wanted to be held, being chosen far more than his share in Duck, Duck, Goose, or cracking on Abarrane when she could not figure out how to turn the shower on, his comic relief was a welcome break from the heart-wrenching trauma the team was witnessing.

God also did a work in me through Joshua. I had never really been comfortable around openly gay individuals, especially men. I had always believed in "Love the sinner, but hate the sin." God showed that statement held a modicum of superiority. We are all sinners! From this trip forward, I have now adopted a new slogan: "Love the sinner, and serve the sinner." I believe this new slogan lines up better with how Jesus would have us feel about people.

The day finished with our first ever Matthew Party, which we held at a local church. We tried to explain the obviously obscure concept to the Haitian ministers, but although they did not understand, they appreciated our effort. When Jesus came to Matthew, Matthew was a tax collector, one of the most despised occupations of the time. The night he left his world behind to follow Jesus, they ended up having dinner at his home. His friends were also looked upon as sinners, and therefore the religious frowned upon the whole scene. They failed to discern that Matthew's guests were the exact people that Jesus came to save. The people who came to our Matthew Party were church members who all came dressed as if they were coming to church. I chuckled as I told the team that we needed to start somewhere! We fed one hundred people for one hundred dollars, including chicken, and created a lot of goodwill toward the pastor, which was both a bargain and a blessing.

The following day was the last full day for the entire team, and I had packed it full. We were welcoming Karen back for the second week to chaperone Kefira and Maya, as Danya would be returning stateside with the rest of the team. Karen's plane had been delayed by several hours; thus, our plans changed on the fly once again. Our first stop was a new all-boys orphanage. The boys loved all the attention, especially from the female team members. The orphanage was clean but way too small, and their outside play area was composed of dirt and rocks. We stayed for about an hour before leaving them food and heading for our next stop.

We had twice as much food to give away on this trip as ever before. I was either finally getting smarter or at least getting better at listening to the prompting of the Holy Spirit. The money for the food outreaches had been raised separately from the trip money, which relieved a great deal of pressure from me. I loved the fact that every dime of the food money came from student donations. Children helping children is a concept that is near and dear to my heart.

The Holy Spirit had impressed on me the need to spend earmarked money only for its intended purpose. Any deviation from this would lead to a loss of credibility and negatively affect God's work in Haiti. This was valuable instruction from the Holy Spirit, which we carried forward into our permanent missionary post assignments. It was a blessing to us and our partners to be able to bring food to every stop we made for the entire trip.

With more time available, we headed to Canaan and the tent city orphanage. This is the poorest orphanage we visit, and it is always in need. We brought food once again and held a medical clinic for the children. There were still clear signs of malnutrition here; however, on this visit the fever caused by the chikungunya virus took precedence. We spent about two hours here, and when it was time to leave, Jenice melted down. She had fallen in love with one of the orphans, Crystal, and could not deal with the thought of leaving her. Jenice's soft, kind heart was now fully exposed as God revealed to us both why she was being trained as a youth leader. The depth of her feeling and her gentleness of spirit were unsurpassed by any on this team.

We next sped to the airport and picked up Karen on our way to the next orphanage, where Valentina lived. Unbeknownst to any of us, the trip was about to take a hard turn south. Each day from this point forward became more of a struggle for me. This was to be the last day that I would see Valentina. The flood of emotions about her departure from the orphanage are still locked and chained away in a room deep within me. Every time the tears attempt to surface, I throw another chain around the room holding my grief.

Her dad had found her, and although he had no visible way to support her, he was going to take her this Sunday. I suggested we offer him money to let her stay where she was, but the orphanage pastor was way ahead of me and had already tried that ploy. At the end of the clinic, I held her close as the team laid hands on her, and we prayed for God's protection and provision for her. Karen, Kefira, and I choked back the tears welling up within us. It was a somber and quick exit as we piled into the van and wove our way back to Gressier. I plugged into my music and tuned out, disconnecting from the rest of the team as I suppressed the grief and pain threatening to engulf me.

I was still not emotionally prepared as we began the evening devotional time and team meeting. The week had flown by, as always, and I was ready to begin the warfare in the mountains. Behaviorally the team showed signs of breaking down the last night. The girls' bathroom looked as if it had been used by drunken sailors on leave, and two of the girls began to fight and yell obscenities at each other. God had showed up in a big way all week in all their lives, and I prayed that they had all been changed for the better.

With that said, the nonbelievers and baby Christians together outnumbered the Spirit-filled Christians two to one, which was clearly not a high enough ratio to maintain spiritual order. There were no surprises during the meeting; rather, there were confirmations of what I had observed. Jenice, Abarrane, and Saul were the most emotional and most distraught about leaving. If there had been an MVP award this week, it would have gone to Saul for his selfless service. It seemed every time I turned around, he was going out of his way to be of service. One evening I had walked into the kitchen in the dark and flipped on the light. There was Saul sitting on the floor filling the whole team's water bottles and returning them to the cooler for the next day. No one else probably even noticed, but God did.

I believed that Joan was also just as blessed as she was a blessing. It was nice having a chaperone who understood what we did and why we were doing it. I prayed that she would be a voice for the children of Haiti when she returned home—and of course I hoped that she would return to Haiti in the future.

The next morning we hustle the team out the door, as most are heading back to America. I am trying to keep my head in the game and my spiritual antennae up, but I am hot, tired, and bombarded by what seems like a billion things that I should not have to be dealing with. We have seen an inordinate amount of funerals this week, which always creates a somber mood within me. On the way to the airport, we pass a man whose head has been run over. This gruesome sight leaves a lasting impression on us all. Before the trip is done, we will see another traffic fatality and corpses riddled with bullets from a shootout with police. Apparently, the police leave the bodies for quite some time as examples to the people of what happens to criminals. On the day of Karen's scheduled departure, we will be turned around because another shooting has backed up traffic for miles. I include these details for a purpose. Haiti is once again going back to its dangerous and unpredictable ways. We should still have no fear while we are serving the Lord; however, precaution needs be part of our preparation for each trip.

We finally roll into Project Eden around ten for an emergency chikungunya-driven clinic; children's Tylenol and worm pills are the norm for today. We ran out of fungal cream earlier in the week and therefore are treating the itching with hydrocortisone cream. We are woefully behind schedule as we head toward the mountains.

We arrive at the River Glace (Ice River) around four thirty in the late afternoon; however, construction delays us for an additional hour and a half. This information was never relayed to us; nor was the fact that we would have to make other arrangements for our last night's stay. Having all information in advance is crucially important in Haiti, and passing along information is definitely a Haitian weakness.

The next morning we drive to Pestel and sail to Billard for their summer clinic. Although the clinics are advertised for children, we are seeing a growing number of adults who want to be treated as well. The clinic goes seamlessly with Karen running the worming station while Kefira and Maya treat the children after I triage them. I sometimes sense that Karen feels she is being punished or at least demeaned by worming the children, but nothing could be further from the truth. The worm pill is crucial for the children's health, and this station slows the flow of traffic to me so I am not inundated with children while attempting to triage them. It is vital to have a strong team member staffing the worm pill station.

We finish the day with a swim at a deserted beach that has become Kefira's and my favorite getaway while in the mountains. Maya quickly falls in love with it as well, as we enjoy a much needed break. The day actually went too well, which should indicate to me that all Hades is about to ascend on us.

That evening we question the pastor as to whether any teams from PaP have been here and whether the feeding programs are continuing. He responds that no teams have come in quite some time but that food is still arriving for Jolie Gilbert, Cayes LaSalle, and Malkushan. With that said, we change the plan for the following day. If we had visited Cayes LaSalle, we would have reignited the silly little ministry war that had begun the previous summer. Instead, we sent food ahead to Cafayier and LeFevre.

Toward the end of our forty-five minute hike through the mountain jungle, we come to the house where we prayed for the dying baby last January. I have fully prepared myself to hear that the baby is dead. The father tells us that two weeks after we left, his wife succumbed to starvation; however, the baby is alive and is at the clinic waiting for us. Encouraged by God's miraculous healing power, we quicken our steps in preparation for the clinic.

No one has ever held a clinic here before, and it is quite obvious. There is no shelter for us, and we end up using a stone wall for a table. The children are loaded with worms, and many show signs of severe malnutrition. One young boy has a compound fracture close to his knee. The doctor has reset it, and he is able to walk, yet something has gone horribly wrong: more than an inch of cartilage protrudes from the back of his knee.

When I first notice the boy, he is perhaps ten meters from me, and I believe I'm seeing infection. I send Maya over to clean it so I can get a better look. The wound is actually covered in maggots, eating the surrounding flesh. Maya begins to wipe them away until the boy winces in pain and begins to cry. Maya has been traumatized enough, so I step in to finish cleaning the wound, pack it with antibiotic cream, and form a gauze tent over the sight. I give his parents a little money to go see the doctor in Pestel, as I am concerned that gangrene may set in.

Maya is still upset, believing that she caused the boy's pain. I take her aside and reassure her with some comforting words that she is doing an amazing job. It is a rough few hours, but the Spirit within keeps us focused and working through the now scorching sun.

Once the clinic ends, we serve the children rice and beans and visit with them until we are out of time. The water ran out hours ago, and the heat is oppressive as we begin our hike out of the mountain jungle. At one juncture, I am so exhausted that I just want to lie down in a hole. I've played sports all my life, and I am used to fatigue, but I have never experienced anything like this before. My ankles are throbbing with pain, although I don't remember twisting them. I assume that the pain results from hiking through the jungle for two days on uneven ground. Little do I suspect that the enemy is already beginning to counterpunch and that I'm feeling the first signs of chikungunya.

———◆━━◆◆◆━━◆———

We were all exhausted as we pulled into Cafayier a little after four. We had brought plenty of food so we were able to feed the adults once the children had been fed. I sent word ahead so my little mountain angel Josie could come and eat and so I could see her and check on her condition. She looked good, and she was going through a growth spurt, at least four inches taller than she had been during our winter mission.

We spent the night in a typical mountain home, which was a first for my team. Once we had eaten a nice dinner, we settled into bed. Soon, a violent and prolonged thunderstorm struck. As it started to rain on my bed, I smiled as I moved my legs around, trying to find a spot where it was not raining. The wind began blowing through the house, causing my mosquito netting to blow out straight rather than hanging perpendicular.

I noticed that the girls' light was on, so I went to check on them. Karen was being attacked. One of her greatest fears is bugs, and their room was loaded with them from the storm. We stayed up with her until the storm subsided and she fell asleep. By morning I had full-fledged chikungunya and was burning with fever. I could not close my left hand, which made opening the bottle of Tylenol a challenge. It took four days for the fever to break and another three before my joint pain decreased to tolerable levels; however, the pain then settled into my ankles and lasted for three more months.

As soon as we arrived back in the United States, Kefira contracted chikungunya as well, leaving none of the mountain team unscathed. She also received a great deal of criticism for a picture that was posted on Facebook of her treating a child without gloves. It was a valuable lesson for me, as she was following my example; even though I instruct them all to wear gloves at all times during the clinics. She never did return to Haiti after that trip, nor did she ever give a reason why.

The next few days are a little blurry; I was fighting fever and incredible pain within my joints. Only through divine grace was I able to continue leading through this period. As I previously mentioned, we were unable to get Karen to the airport for her scheduled departure. I decided to flip our itinerary days and spend the day at Project Eden, once again assisting with prison ministry in Petit-Goâve (Ti Gwav).

The following morning we were finally able to get Karen on her plane. We then decided to visit the mass grave entombing the remains of the victims of the 2010 earthquake that was located just north of Canaan. They had recently walled and gated the site to try to protect it from looters, but to no avail. Inside should have stood one hundred thousand small wooden crosses, but as we peered through the bars, none were in sight. Undaunted by the bars, Maya squeezed through, followed by Kefira. I found this quite amusing, since not even my leg would fit through the bars. My young leaders spent a long while wandering the site and could not describe how they felt other than they were glad we had taken the time to visit. Since this trip, beautiful monuments and gardens have been created here in memory of the victims. Armed guards secure the entrance but are more than gracious hosts when visitors come to pay their respects to those buried here.

We then traveled back into the city to visit the American orphanage. We were privileged to receive a tour from a very nice young pastor, who had been raised here as a child. The new boys' dormitory was near completion, and I expected it would be full of children by my next visit. We were supposed to visit Cité Soleil for a short outreach and so that my leaders might see the mud cakes being made; however, once Maya said that she was not scared and wanted to go, the Holy Spirit removed the desire for me to take them there. I felt the need to know what we were capable of doing on this trip so I could plan future trips appropriately. I also needed to know how far I could push Maya. Was she really ready to step into Kefira's shoes as the new leader? Once I knew the answer was yes, the reason for going was removed, and the risk far outweighed the benefit. If God wanted us to hold a significant outreach there, then it would happen on a future trip.

Friday was our day off, and we spent much of it at the Port Royal Hotel in Ti Gwav. We enjoyed the cool pool water and a relaxed poolside patio lunch. My fever had finally broken, and the pain focused primarily in my ankles. Later that afternoon, we stopped to help the California sorority team, as they had broken down on their way to our former compound. God's timing is impeccable!

Several days before, we had stopped twice more, once to change a flat tire and the other time to assist missionaries whom the police were extorting. Extortion is a common practice at the all-too-common Haitian police roadblocks. When we lived in Haiti full-time, we were stopped almost on a daily basis. After about the sixth time of being extorted, I explained that my wife and I were missionary pastors and did not have much money; what money we did have, we used to feed and care for the Haitian children. After that, the officers would only ask for prayer, which I was more than happy to provide.

Although partially refreshed from our day off, we were still emotionally exhausted the next day. We were excited that Pastor M would be chaperoning my young leaders for the last six days, and I was even more excited to be with my wife after two and a half grueling weeks of ministry. I hoped and prayed that she would give the team the lift of energy they needed to complete our last six days strong. We were once again visiting a very poor orphanage, as it was a great way to get restarted. The children were starved for attention, and any love we offered was immediately lapped up. We were hosting a large team for the remainder of our stay in Haiti, and I was anything but excited. The adrenaline of ministry waned as we overloaded two vehicles and headed for our mission house in Gressier. The overloaded truck overheated on the way. We packed the visiting team into the one running vehicle and brought them to the guesthouse while our staff remained with the truck.

It took Pastor M two days to readjust to Haiti, and Kefira and Maya seemed apathetic and lethargic. They had both started their monthly cycles, and although they were neither rude nor unpleasant, the change in them was obvious. Although these six days were a struggle for us, God continued to use us as a blessing. In between serving our guests, we were able to hold a hot dog feeding in Grand Goave at Project Eden and feed the prisoners one final time. On Sunday I preached a strong message, and afterward, the church treated the team to a feast.

The pastor asked for help paying his workers, as he had run out of money. I told him that I would see what we had left at the end of our mission; however, it had cost nearly one thousand dollars to host the visiting team plus the truck repairs. As we neared the end of our time, I realized we were going to be out of money. As I prayed, I felt released to give the pastor our weekly tithe, an amount that nearly covered what he had asked for.

We spent much of our remaining time at our former compound. The California sorority was staying there, which made for some very hectic visits. There is a great need for parental figures at our former compound, and Pastor M and I had entered into prayer to see if God would have us step into that role.

On our way back to Gressier, we passed an old blind man named Bonbass. My first reaction was to feel sorry for him, as it usually is when I see someone with any kind of disability. I do not understand why disabilities create an uneasy feeling within me. I am fully cognizant of the fact that obstacles are character builders placed to make us stronger for a purpose set long before we were conceived. Just as I was about to divert my stare, he looked me straight in the eyes as if he could see within me. I was momentarily unnerved; it took a minute for me to hear the still small voice whispering, *Bless him with some money.* I had hoped to hear the Holy Spirit's voice more on this mission, so we clearly had one more assignment.

We pulled a sharp U-turn, raising a cloud of dust, as we began looking for him. We caught him about a half a mile down the road. We told him we wanted to bless him with some money and asked if he would like prayer. I believe his knees hit the ground before we were even finished speaking. He extended his hands toward heaven as he looked up and then just as quickly bowed his head to the ground as we laid hands on him and prayed. This was a great final blessing and reminder for us concerning who is in charge and who we are here to serve and glorify.

I felt that we were finally done with our mission as I nodded off on one last drive, but God had one more piece of service awaiting us. That evening the leader of the team we were hosting asked Pastor M and me to share our story with his team. We had come to like this team, and apparently they felt the same way.

God has an incredible way of teaching me not to be judgmental. We learned that this team was the core of a familiar ministry. This was the ministry that asked us not to put a village water filtration system in Malkushan because they had already given out family-sized units there. I also learned that two years before, while staying at the American compound in PaP, I had met members of this team, and we had enjoyed some pleasant conversations together.

Pastor M and I shared how we ended up ministering in Haiti and our great love for her children. Later we learned how moved and inspired members of their team were by our testimony. We never know whom we will touch by simply being obedient to the voice of the Holy Spirit.

Overall, this was an incredibly blessed trip with many remarkable and miraculous moments. I learned many valuable lessons and was reminded of others that God had already shown me but that I had forgotten. I also received a thrashing physically, emotionally, and mentally. It took months of nightly soaking to relieve the throbbing pain in my ankles. Kefira's parents would most likely prefer that she not return, and perhaps she is a little discouraged as well.

Despite all the pain and turmoil within me, we had accomplished the four goals that I had set for this trip. The majority of the team had a burning desire to return and serve again. Kefira and I had initiated Maya into the war here, and she was outstanding. What other two teenage girls would go out tarantula hunting in the dark? I now knew that our ministry limit was three outreaches a day for two weeks before we reached the point of exhaustion. Finally, we had accomplished the most important goal, which was leaving everything we had in Haiti. We were God's hands and feet as we poured every single ounce of love and energy we had into Haiti's little ones. For once in my life, I could truly say that I had no more to give.

There were still thousands of children at risk within our reach. Nevertheless, for now, I prayed only for God's refreshing and renewal because I still felt like a toy soldier. Perhaps we had missed the most exquisite part of God's mission in Haiti. Maybe, just maybe, it was not the Haitians that God wanted us to save but ourselves.

I am not certain if a person can have borderline PTSD, but I certainly exhibited many of the signs during that time frame. By this time the chikungunya had settled in my ankles, and even a few steps were quite painful. My nightmares became more vivid and more frequent. Valentina was gone, and Kefira and Sela were now on their way to college. I had not heard from Maya all summer, and she was not there when school began. I grew despondent when I was unable to schedule a fall mission to Haiti.

At my bleakest moment, Saul came into my classroom and asked if I had heard from Maya. He was trying to hold back a smirk, and she shortly burst into the room. I was overjoyed to see her. Over the next week, we planned an aggressive fundraising and outreach schedule as well as mission trips for January, March, and June.

Miryam had been a wonderful mentor for Kefira, and Kefira was a wonderful mentor to Maya. There was a difference, though, as I had personally helped in Maya's mentorship. She was now so much like me it was scary. We raised more money and helped more people in the fall than we ever had in a whole year.

During the winter mission, Abarrane and Saul became ill just before our largest clinic in LeFevre. Danya ran the worming station, and I triaged, which left Maya by herself to treat over five hundred children. That clinic was the pinnacle of our achievement but also marked the end of a season for my teen disciples.

In His love,

Pastor D

My Dearest Macy and Mark,

You will soon become the hands and feet of Jesus. This is a huge blessing and responsibility. The level to which you embrace your call will be the measure of your success in the field. You will have very little control over most of your life in the field; however, you have complete control over your attitude when it comes to those God brings you. The Invisible Child marks a transition in our journey from our old life of serving part-time to our new life of twenty-four-hour-per-day service. The transition process was not easy for us. We completed two years of Bible school in one year. We were ripped away from everything we knew and sequestered like Elijah in our own personal Kerith Ravine.

Once our training was complete, we zigzagged the country, speaking at numerous churches to gain our monthly support for our mission. This was a difficult process, as we had always raised our own money for our needs. Learning to trust God's plan and His provision was difficult; however, in the eleventh hour, God always showed up in a big way. Once in-country, we lived like pioneers at first with no electricity or running water. We carried water for our needs several times per day and kept our food from spoiling by purchasing ice from a neighboring town. Although basic survival took a larger portion of our day, we were so glad to be on the ground in Haiti serving that we simply did not mind.

Lesson 15: Become the Hands and Feet of Jesus

The Invisible Child

As we begin preparations for next week's team trip, I find myself wading through a flood of emotions. God is working on me as the turmoil and conflicts continue to rage. I wish I really had full control of my flesh; that would certainly reduce the conflicts within my spirit. I see in my mind's eye the "Mountain of Death" near Pestel. I feel the anxiety mounting as anticipation for my summer trip builds, so close yet still so far away. I picture the lost souls, the hunger, and the diseased children. Almost virgin ground, removed from civilization as we know it, with little hope of tomorrow, let alone a brighter tomorrow. I am not so gently reminded by the Holy Spirit that these are not the only lost and suffering souls.

She times her entrance as the bell rings to start first period. Although the temperature will most likely be close to ninety today, she is wearing an oversized hooded sweatshirt with jeans at least one size too small. She slinks into her seat, and then in a moment, slouches down, hood up and headphones hidden, as another school day begins. She rolls her eyes as I ask her to remove her headphones, but she complies without a confrontation.

The students have been earning an abundance of zeros as the final quarter is quickly ending. I decide to abandon today's lesson in hopes that by giving them a little extra time I may see some of their missing work. A few more minutes pass, and I decide it's now safe to take attendance as the stragglers have most likely all made it in.

Although I noticed her coming through the door, I really did not see her and thus must check her seat to make sure she is present. She has now been my student for thirty-eight weeks and I cannot recall what her voice sounds like or even if I have ever heard it. She earns mostly D grades and seldom higher than a C. I have never seen a smile on her face, as she usually appears uninterested and apathetic. I make a pass around the room and notice that she has written her name on her paper but nothing else. I think about talking with her and encouraging her, but I had her boyfriend last year, and no matter how hard I tried, I could not get him to pass. She is guilty by association.

An A student raises their hand and I gladly go over to assist them. Then a corrective behavior needs to be addressed. An announcement comes over the intercom, once again disturbing everyone's train of thought. I settle the class back into their work. I have already forgotten about the girl, and I return to my desk to wade through the endless stack of paperwork.

It is now minutes before the end of class. I wrap up the day's work with the students and preview the next class. I am not sure if she hears because her head is now on the desk. The bell rings, and the students exit, most bringing me work; I wish them all a nice day as I prepare for more of the same.

She exits as quietly as she entered, looking more like an automaton than a young woman. As she exits, I see her for the first time as the Holy Spirit quickens me. Has she eaten? Is the hood being used to hide bruises? Is she pregnant? Has she lost a loved one? Does she live in a loveless home surrounded by constant verbal abuse? As time passes, I will forget her name. Eventually, her face will fade from my memory. If I do not act soon, I will lose the chance to influence this child in a positive way.

How many hurting and lost children do I walk by each and every day? I do not see them because I am in a hurry to get to my destination, and my vision is blurred by the quagmire and futility that the American public school system has become. I would never walk by a child in Haiti without giving them attention, yet I walk by thousands every day here and do not even glance at them. They truly are invisible.

I was never really able to help this young girl the way I had hoped. However, if your heart is in the right place, God has a way of rectifying areas where you have fallen short. Two years later, I had the opportunity to teach her sister. I took no chances from day one when I placed her right in front of my desk while creating the seating chart. This placement helps develop rapport with students so when they run into difficulties, personal or academic, they tend to ask for assistance. The plan worked perfectly, as she quickly rose to become one of the top students that year.

Fast-forward an additional three years into the future. The children are still invisible; however, here they do not hide under hoods and headsets. No, here they are actually quite invisible, buried deep within fields or high up on mountainsides. Each week we venture farther from the roads and deeper into the unknown wilderness. Some of Haiti's most beautiful locations are found by simply driving off road. Our favorite spot can only be reached by driving through a narrow mountain pass with a thousand-foot drop on either side. Normally I would not risk such an adventure without the reward of helping children; however, the sunsets on this ridge are truly breathtaking and have helped renew us as we revel in God's glorious creation.

Most days it is obvious that the enemy hates us, and his constant barrage of half-truths must be squelched daily. The relentless sweltering heat makes his lies seem more plausible as the day weighs heavy upon us. The plethora of insurmountable problems adds credence to his lies: "You're not making a difference; no one really cares; everything and everyone you love is back home. He doesn't really love you."

It is simply the still small voice that keeps us going, pushing harder to do more each and every day for more and more children. "Therefore go and make disciples of all nations, baptizing them in the name of the Father and of the Son and of the Holy Spirit, and teaching them to obey everything I have commanded you" (Matthew 28:19–20). First, let us be quite clear: the word *go* does not imply a choice; it is most definitely a command. Second, to actually accomplish the rest of this command in the fourth world, one must also live out the Parable of the Sheep and the Goats found in Matthew 25. If a child is hungry, thirsty, unhealthy, unclothed, or unsafe in their home, then fulfilling the Great Commission is nearly impossible simply because no one is listening.

So to the enemy of our souls: We would agree with you. We are not making a difference, because what is happening is surely not us. Hundreds if not thousands of children now scream out our names. Children we do not know end up on our doorstep, hungry, sick, and unclothed, and we help them. For years now, I have told people who want to come to Haiti but feel they have nothing worth bringing that the most important thing they bring is the love of Jesus within them. Yes, today I will feed children; however, more importantly, I will hug children and tell them that Jesus loves them, and so do we. We bring the hope, the love, and the light of Christ into the darkness. It is not we who find the invisible children; it is He who guides our steps to them.

In His love,
Pastor D

My Dearest Macy and Mark,

Today I would like to broach a subject that I believe is essential to success in missions. As a teenager, I began the practice of watching people new to my circle. My intent was to see what type of person they were before befriending them. This tendency did not ever completely disappear; it shifted and altered as I matured. I can be friends with many diverse types of people, literally from any background or ethnic group. However, I intuitively search for those with a kindred heart, those who value love and mercy over judgment and strict adherence to religious dogma.

As missionaries, we must hold ourselves to high standards and continuously strive for sanctification, but we cannot hold those we serve to those same standards. We can teach and correct in love, but never should we apply judgment to those we serve. As we begin to explore what God has for us in Africa, I am confident in those who lead us there because of this one principle. They had the opportunity to judge someone very close to them but instead showed mercy and compassion. It was not their position or titles that convinced me that they were the ones the Holy Spirit wanted us to collaborate with; it was the mercy they showed, even though it potentially reflected badly on them.

Lesson 16: Mercy over Judgment

Teaching high school is much like being a missionary in the sense that it requires dedication, patience, and an abundance of mercy. During the course of my tenure, I taught at three different schools with three very different student dynamics. I first taught at one of the richest Catholic high schools in the state, followed by the poorest minority school in the state, and finally ended up right in the middle, teaching at a school with the most diverse population in the county. Many teachers used strict rules and adhered to them religiously. I refer to them as the Pharisees of the modern educational system and they are usually well liked by administrators. I on the other hand always maintained order through rapport. My students knew that I loved them and so did not want to disappoint me—at least most of the time. This allowed me to access areas of their lives that others could not reach, but it required great amounts of trust that led to several interesting scenarios over the years.

On one occasion a boy exposed himself in class; I was a novice teacher at the time and, not wanting to get him in trouble, went to his priest rather than the administration. Needless to say, they were not pleased when they found out. They gave me a scolding, but its effect was the opposite of what they expected. Instead of coming to them with every little offense, I simply avoided them completely. Over the course of twenty-two years I probably wrote less than twenty referrals, while other teachers wrote that many in a week.

One honors anatomy and physiology class decided that they would have some fun with me during our yearly cat dissections. I used the restroom between classes, which gave them time to set up a mini ER. They were fully dressed in medical attire and had an oxygen mask hooked to their cat along with an IV running. When I reentered the classroom, they were beginning open heart massage. All I could do was shake my head and laugh.

I also wanted to coach sports, as I had played so many through the years. I was offered the head soccer position; one sport I had hardly ever played. I looked to heaven and thought, *Really*. However, God knew what the future held. I was extremely successful over the course of the first seven years until I transferred to the poorest, almost all-minority school in the Glades. When soccer began, I literally had to show them a soccer ball and explain what it was. The girls' team had never won a game in the school's history, and it was easy to see why. Early in the season, we were slaughtered and mercy-ruled in every game, but I never gave up. We had one advantage over the other teams; my girls were crazy fast.

I adopted a philosophy whereby we would bypass the skilled players of the opposing midfield and play through balls to our forwards. I worked diligently with the forwards to teach them how to shoot on frame. The strategy worked, and we started scoring goals until it finally happened and we won our first game. With all the trophies and awards I won coaching soccer, I was never as happy as I was in that moment.

Through it all, my wife was a faithful team mom, and my children learned to love the game and played throughout their childhood and teen years. I was disappointed with what God had initially given me; however, soccer is the number one sport in the world and now I have an immediate point of mutual interest and connection wherever I go. My team consisted of almost exclusively black players in a white dominated sport. I would not have traded the laughs and loves for a state championship. When they saw Pastor M for the first time, they asked me who she was after I had given her a kiss. I said she was my girlfriend but not to tell my wife. They laughed and joked for the next half hour.

On another occasion they were imitating my assistant coach and me. In a soft melodic tone, they began to imitate my assistant: "It's okay, girls. I know we're down by nine goals, but just have fun." After I stopped laughing they started on me, gruffly yelling: "What's up, Ruth? Why can't you catch the ball?" This was the first time this middle-class white boy who grew up in a virtually all-white state had the opportunity to work with minority kids, and I absolutely loved it.

Eventually the drive became too much and I transferred to an inner city school with a mixed population of approximately equal numbers of black, white, and Hispanic students. During one of my first years there, I taught a young girl who was somewhat misbehaved but was obviously seeking attention. I always tried to be patient with her because it was apparent that she had few friends. One day as I exited my classroom, I heard noise coming from the stairwell. I opened the door to find her on her knees with six other upperclassmen surrounding her waiting their turn. They all ran when I opened the door, and as teens will, they immediately began to tell everyone of her actions. Her parents immediately withdrew her from school, and I never saw her again, but I always felt compassion for her simply because she longed to be liked.

Shortly after we joined our current church, God began to change us. We began serving in assorted church ministries until at one point we were either leading or involved in eleven different ministries. This was about the time that I began to teach chemistry. As the year progressed, I found students who reminded me of myself in high school: smart, underachieving, and bored. I decided to begin an informal club to teach them the value of serving others. Each year the club grew and became better at raising support and serving the neediest among us.

One day one of my students was wearing a hood, and she was using a hand to cover part of her face. After several glances at her during class, I decided to keep her after class and discovered she had a black eye and bruised cheek, apparently a result of her father disciplining her. It was a mess, because legally I had no choice but to call the Department of Children and Families. She joined the club shortly thereafter and grew close to both Pastor M and myself. I had the privilege of baptizing her and another club member that spring.

Eventually she ran away from home. She called me instead of her parents, to let us know that she was all right. Of course I immediately picked up the phone and called her mother; after that, we lost touch for a while. When I next heard from her, she was married with her first baby on the way. Teenagers have a way of growing up; the question then becomes who is guiding their maturation?

During the third year of the club, we began our mission to Haiti, and nine months later the first students went on a Haiti mission trip. The club ran for six years and raised close to fifty thousand dollars for the neediest among us, both here in the States and in Haiti. Over the years, a dozen students had the chance to serve the Haitian children, with most returning for later trips.

In each step of our journey leading to full-time mission work, God was preparing us and changing our hearts. Along the way, I was blessed with many awards and accolades that now simply collect dust. They were merely markers of the stepping-stones God was having us climb. Teaching afforded me the opportunity to mentor and love deeply; however, learning to be merciful was my greatest achievement. As you prepare for the field, please keep this in mind: Mercy should always triumph over judgment!

In His love,

Pastor D

My Dearest Macy and Mark,

I would like to begin with an apology for setting you up. Your presentation of the events that transpired in the Garden of Gethsemane was both thoughtful and thorough; however, it was not quite factual. Your explanation was similar to what most of us are taught through catechism, Sunday school, and even from many pulpits. The firmness with which we believe something to be true does not make it so. Let us take a closer look at Matthew 26:36–46.

Lesson 17: Layers of Truth in God's Word

Gethsemane

When Jesus asks His Father to "let this cup pass from Me" we make a very human assumption. We assume that He is speaking about the humiliation, the horrific scourging, and the inhumane death He will suffer during His crucifixion. We make this assumption based upon two definite premises: first, because we have been taught this by men and women of God, and second, because of our human frailty. If we knew we were about to be treated in this manner, we would be begging God to find an alternate path.

Before we unpack the truth of Gethsemane, let us look at the place itself. Gethsemane was home to an olive press surrounded by a grove of olive trees. The olive press works by squeezing the oil and water from the olive paste. The fibrous parts are discarded, and the liquid mixture is decanted, separating the oil from the water. We will return to the significance of this shortly.

Jesus plainly tells us in verse 38 what is transpiring. "My soul is exceedingly sorrowful, even to death. Stay and watch with Me." Looking at the original Greek version, we may find a little more clarity. "My breath is very sad until death abide here to be awake." In reality, the pressure of Gethsemane was weighing so heavily upon Jesus and His sorrow was so intense that He was having difficulty breathing. It was this extreme pressure that caused Him to sweat tears of blood as He prayed. This condition is termed *hematidrosis*, in which capillaries that feed the sweat glands rupture, causing them to exude blood; this occurs under conditions of extreme physical or emotional stress.

The pressure of Gethsemane is the cup Jesus asked to have removed, not the cross! This is hugely significant, since it clearly demonstrates that

Jesus's great love for us caused Him to never stray from His mission to wash our sins away and restore our relationship with the Father. He was born to go to the cross and never once doubted His mission.

Imagine Jesus sitting on His throne at the right hand of the Father. He says, "It is time," as he stands, removing His crown and laying down His scepter. He takes one more look around at His home in heaven.

Just before He leaves, His Father reaches out and grabs His hand, saying, "I will miss you, Son." We seldom consider the anguish Jesus felt from simply leaving heaven.

We see several other important things happening within the Garden. First, He chooses Peter, James, and John to come with Him. They are His inner circle, His closest confidants; however, He chooses them not for those reasons, but because they all have the gift of mercy. He wants them to commiserate with Him and pray for Him. When Jesus finds them asleep, He says, "Watch and pray, lest you enter into temptation. The spirit indeed is willing, but the flesh is weak." Here He is speaking both to the disciples and prophetically to us, to all who believe in Him.

The other very interesting and applicable aspect of Gethsemane is the change in Jesus's prayers. There is an acceptance growing through the three times He prayed, culminating with an angel of the Lord strengthening Jesus. In verse 46, Jesus, now fully prepared, says, "Rise, let us be going. See, My betrayer is at hand."

I promised that we would return to the significance and symbolism of the olive press ultimately separating the oil and the water. Christ's fortitude over the pressure of Gethsemane leads us to the victory found in the crucifixion. When the Roman soldier sees that Jesus is dead, he does not break His legs, fulfilling the prophetic word that the sacrificial Passover lamb shall have no broken bones (Numbers 9:12). Instead, he uses a spear; thus, we see that when Jesus's side was pierced blood and water poured forth. The blood symbolizes the redemption that washes our sin away, while the water is symbolic, representing the impartation of new life. We were once dead in our sin, but now not only has our sin been washed away, but we have been given new life in Jesus.

When the Lord sent us into our desert to prepare us for a life of missions, I experienced days of such sorrow that I could not breathe. I thought I would die from the oppressive weight of this sorrow, and on more than one occasion, the enemy tried to convince me to take my life. This culminated one sleepless night with an excruciating, deafening crescendo; a fierce battle was being waged between the angelic and demonic for my soul. Gethsemane demonstrates Christ's love and understanding of the great sorrows we experience here. I can never hope to repay Him for what He did for me; my only recompense is to love and serve Him and His children to the best of my ability.

May you both always remember that you are not alone! When the weight of the sorrow in the field becomes so heavy that you have trouble breathing, know that He understands what you are feeling and that His compassion and peace are available to you during every moment.

In His love,

Pastor D

My Dearest Macy and Mark,

There will be times when you will give all you have and it simply will not be enough. Other times, you will have incredible victories against seemingly insurmountable odds. You must learn that doing your best is all you can do. With the correct perspective, failure can also bring glory to God. In the big picture, the outcome is less important than the process. This is a hard pill for us to swallow as humans, especially when it concerns the life and death of children.

I have thought about Tamara almost every day for the past three years. She is one I will look for when I am taken to heaven. It is perfectly acceptable to grieve and mourn; however, it is equally unacceptable to let failure and fear retard your process of growing in the Lord and serving His people.

Lesson 18: Your Best Is All You Can Give

Fathers Shouldn't Have to Bury Their Daughters

Early Easter afternoon I was told a young girl was very sick who lived just up the hill from the twins. As I grabbed the medical bag and prepared to leave, the Holy Spirit quickened me to the fact that neither my wife nor our intern should come with me. The instant I saw Tamara, I was gravely concerned. She had been vomiting for eight days continually, unable to keep down any food or liquids. She was running a mid-grade fever, and her breathing was rapid and shallow. She was ridiculously thin for her age; however, the severe malnourishment and dehydration of her tiny body could have easily contributed to this appearance.

I so wish that I had gotten to her sooner! The first hospital she went to sent her home with Amoxicillin and iron-fortified vitamins. I immediately gave the father a thousand gourdes and told him to take her back to the hospital and not leave until they were able to stop the vomiting. She crawled into my lap as I wrapped my arms around her to pray and comfort her. She was looking at me with her soft brown eyes that were pleading for help. I gave her liquid fever reducer, which she almost immediately vomited back up. We laid hands on her, pleading the blood of Christ over her; we then drove into town to buy some Gatorade and get her filtered water to rehydrate her. Unfortunately, our efforts were too little, too late. Tamara, age ten, died in the early evening of Resurrection Sunday and is now dancing with Jesus.

Today the vision that haunted me for the last three days became manifest as I brought Tamara's dad into the mortuary to help pay for her final expenses. You could literally feel the freezer's cold and eerie pitch-blackness as we entered. Suddenly, the funeral director's phone light came on and a rainbow of colors glimmered off Tamara's naked, frozen, emaciated, Popsicle like corpse. On the verge of losing it, I immediately shut down emotionally as her father loudly and uncontrollably began to wail.

We were happy to give the little we could to help Mr. Pierre. Just before I pulled away, while he was profusely thanking me, he told me that the day I sent Tamara to the hospital he only had five gourdes to his name. In US currency five gourdes is the equivalent of three cents. Mr. Pierre still owed six hundred dollars; it might as well have been six million. We celebrated Tamara's life the next Sunday at Good Seed Church. It was a very difficult day for all simply because fathers should not have to bury their daughters.

Several months later, Mr. Pierre came to our home panicked. His eldest daughter Pauline, was now gravely ill. Her symptoms were much like Tamara's. We brought her to our home and began the process of rehydrating her and bringing down her fever. Her fever broke after a few hours, and Mr. Pierre decided to bring her home. A couple of days later he came back to our home even more frantic than he was the first time. Apparently, Pauline had relapsed, and her relatives had taken her to the local witch doctor's home. I was immediately convicted and determined that Mr. Pierre would not have to bury another daughter. Although highly risky, we drove to the witch doctor's house, burst through the front door, scooped Pauline from the dining table, and quickly loaded her into my SUV before speeding away. Over the next few days, I hiked up the hill to her home three times a day, bringing her medicine and healthy meals. Within a few days, she made a full recovery, returning to school in PaP a few weeks later.

If it had not been for Tamara's untimely demise, I am not sure if I would have been so proactively aggressive in my pursuit of Pauline's care. The one thing I know for sure is that fathers should not have to bury their daughters!

In His love,

Pastor D

My Dearest Macy and Mark,

As you are now fully engaged in your final year of preparation, I have a suggestion for you both. If I were you, I would seriously consider marriage before you are commissioned to your missionary post. I realize that your generation views marriage differently than mine; however, you are Christ's ambassadors, and as such you will be scrutinized much more than you can now fathom.

In addition, Macy, your position as a female missionary will be far more influential as a married woman. Married women will have more respect for you, and single women will be more apt to turn to you for advice. The children will look at you as a maternal figure, and the men will be less inclined to attempt to solicit sex from you. Being married will also enhance your position, Mark, and offer you increased credibility and respect among the local church.

You will have enough battles because you are foreigners. You do not need to add being single and living together to your fight. No one will believe that you are celibate in your relationship, which will totally negate your ability to speak concerning matters of relationship and sexual intimacy.

Lesson 19: Oneness in the Sight of God

And Then They Were One

Have you ever felt that there must be something more, maybe even that you were meant for something great, unusual, or extraordinary? Have you ever wondered what living in God's perfect will would be like? I did! For years, decades actually, I lived in God's permissive will. Although when I was a young Christian, He had shown me His supernatural power, perhaps unwittingly, I choose the normal and safe path. You know the path I mean: the one where being just slightly better than those around you is acceptable. Why step out of the boat to be the best when above average is so comfortable?

God literally snatched me from the jaws of death in my early-twenties. Heavy drinking and an acute fondness for cocaine left me wondering if life really had any purpose other than to perpetuate our species. I knew there had to be more to life than working and partying with my friends.

One of my friends and coworkers invited me to church. My church experience had consisted of an occasional visit to Catholic church on either Christmas or Easter. This church was fully Pentecostal and nothing like I had ever experienced before. When people started going out in the Spirit, I grew frightened, almost frantic to leave before they passed out the poisoned juice as had happened in Jamestown. After about four months and a lot of persuasion, my friend finally convinced me to give the church a second try. This time the Holy Spirit met me in a big way, and I was soon saved.

Shortly after my salvation, God began to show me glimpses of His power. When I was still a young boy, an angel had visited me at night. I knew he was an angel, and I felt a combination of fear and peace. The fear side won, and I pulled the covers over my head until he left. As a young adult, I had rested in the Spirit several times; however, being slain in the

Spirit is a very different experience. I was present in both the corporeal and spiritual worlds and not really in control of anything in either one. One thing was for certain, I could not bring myself out of this state myself, even though I tried several times before I surrendered to the Holy Spirit.

How hungry I was for the things of God as a baby Christian—quite literally ingesting all the knowledge and experience I could grasp. It was then that God gave me the ability to see into the Spirit world. I joined a very active and spiritually aggressive young adults' group. One night we were engaged in a particularly aggressive spiritual warfare intercession when I saw scores of demons surrounding us at the windows. Instead of pressing in closer to God, I became afraid and begged God to remove the gift He gave me; He immediately granted my request. What I had failed to glean was that fear was complicity with Satan's plan. This was a lesson that took decades to really learn.

Next, I believed that as a young Christian man in my mid to late twenties, I should have a wife, and for that matter, I should help God select her. I proceeded to select a number of what I felt were good candidates, to which God simply replied, *"No."* Showing a great deal of Christian maturity, I got frustrated and a little angry with God and said, "Fine, I'll just stay single then."

Shortly after this God told me that Pastor M would be my wife, I threw the biggest hissy fit ever: "No, not the hugging girl!" I was so distraught that I left the state to visit my family in New Jersey. While there, God temporarily removed the knowledge of His revelation. I returned to Vermont and several months passed uneventfully. We did not know until much later that Pastor P, who was a prophetess, had turned to her husband Pastor T and said that I was Pastor M's husband the very first time I had visited the church.

On September 30, 1988, we went out on our first date; it was by far the worst first date either of us had been on. I was ultraconservative, the kind of person who would watch you for two weeks to make sure that I really wanted to speak with you. Pastor M, on the other hand, was extremely outgoing. As we stood in line to see *Mississippi Burning*, arguably the worst first date movie ever made, she was jumping up and down over the crowd to say hi to someone fifty feet in front of us. As we pulled up to her apartment, she had the door open and was halfway out before the car stopped. She turned and asked me to a dinner party at her house that

Sunday, to which I said yes. Neither of us knew why this happened because we both had an awful time and really did not want to see each other again. The dinner party was awesome; we laughed and had great food and great fun, which really broke the ice between us.

Pastor M wanted to get into shape, so the first week I agreed to train her. We found that we had so much in common that by the second week we were dating casually. The third week we became exclusive to each other, and by the fifth week we were engaged and went to visit my parents in New Jersey. We set a June wedding date but quickly realized we would not be able to wait that long to consummate our union. The Saturday that began our seventh week together, I selected matching three colored gold rings and headed toward Pastor M's salon. I asked if she was serious about getting married early. When she replied yes, I said, "How about Thursday?" We had a beautiful intimate ceremony in front of her parents' fireplace with thirty close friends, family, and our pastors.

Many thought our marriage would not last, but God certainly knew what we needed. I have known from very early that we were perfect complements. Where she is weak, I am strong, and vice versa. When we are functioning in God's will, we are simply unstoppable. She has a huge heart and an incredible desire to serve others. I cannot imagine life without my wife, my lover, and my best friend. We raised three awesome children and have eight beautiful grandbabies so far, with another on the way. We are one in God's eyes and I have just begun to understand the full implications of that statement. This is not to say everything was a joyride; no, far from it. We have been battered and beaten down several times, but we hang on tight to each other and to God during the tough times.

We now live in the fourth world and dedicate ourselves as full-time missionaries serving God's little ones. We go places and do things that only a few would believe and even fewer would join in. We are fiercely loyal to all those we love and look forward with great expectancy and anticipation for God's next steps. Real life was never meant to be ordinary or mundane. God has a great and perfect plan for you both if you will just let go and let God! I pray my testimony helps give you clarity and direction as you pray concerning this extremely important decision.

In His love,

Pastor D

My Dearest Macy and Mark,

Today I would like to take some time discussing who gets the credit and accolades for what we do. The answer is obviously God. God forbid that you ever get to the point where you think you deserve anything. No one needs another pair of silk pajamas or a fleet of limousines. Give God the glory, and He will always have you in the palm of His hand.

Lesson 20: The Glory Belongs to God

Without Pomp and Circumstance

Year seven of our work in Haiti has begun most inauspiciously, more than likely because life here is hectic and intense and often not easy. There are countless pathogens that cause intestinal distress, and we seem to have found most of them, although my penchant for street food does not help matters much. Most days it is ridiculously hot, and spiritual warfare is literally a constant and ongoing reality. Recently, we buried five people in the span of five months; the last two were children who died tragically and needlessly. I have walked the streets of Cité Soleil and watched as the mud cookies baked in the sun, meant to quell the cries of the children on the verge of starvation's death. We have known children who were sold, molested, and discarded like trash. We have seen people murdered before our very eyes and witnessed firsthand the glowing red eyes of the demonically possessed. I have endured months of nightmares of both the faces of the starving children and the dead. Ten thousand flaming arrows of the enemy have hit me. I have been mad at God and even called Him a liar to His face. I have hurt everyone I loved and betrayed myself. I have felt the grip of sorrow's grasp so tight I was unable to breathe and felt as if we'd been cast into the desert of despair and anguish, where the only thing to drink was an endless sea of unquenchable tears. When I close my eyes, I still see the rainbow of color shimmering from Tamara's naked, frozen corpse; perhaps I always will.

If you are reading this for the first time, you may be thinking, "Dude, why are you doing this to yourself?" The answer is quite simple. To know the sovereignty of God and witness the power of God, you must be willing to follow God wherever He leads. We have seen the dead raised, incredible healings, and children who could not possibly live flourishing in His presence. We have cast out demons in His name and watched as Jesus freed and saved the captive. We have had the incredible privilege of walking out Matthew 25:35–40 daily. Through mandated initiatives, we have seen thousands given medical care and tens of thousands of children wormed and fed. God has granted us incredible favor and dominion in our community and the nearby communities in which we serve. We get to walk among the people daily and pour out incredible amounts of His love on them. We get to hug, care for, and love on what seems an endless multitude of children. We have been afforded the incredible blessing of being able to live like apostles and serve in God's great adventure.

To those whom we have served with, bled with, cried with, and most definitely laughed with, we are awaiting your return. God is not fickle; once you are a warrior, a leader, or a disciple, you will always be welcome, wanted, and most of all loved. To those of you we have yet to serve with, come on ahead; we are waiting for you. One day a couple of months ago a little boy pointed at me and said, "Jesus." I was able to hold it together until I finished what I was doing. Driving home, I had to pull over to weep because I was the only Jesus this boy knew. The incredible magnitude and awesomeness of what God has called us to do hit me like a ton of bricks: what kind of Jesus am I? I am reminded of Philippians 1:21: "For to me, to live is Christ and to die is gain." Without Christ, I am no kind of Jesus at all!

Shortly after this event, God once again showed Himself sovereign as I led a small team into the mountains for our semiannual medical clinics. We were blessed with smooth and productive clinics at both Cafayier and Billard.

We spent the night at our favorite guesthouse in Pestel with the hope of heading to LeFevre the next morning. We learned that the proprietor was recovering in the hospital after a car accident. Managing her B and B was a very attractive, well-educated Haitian woman with a commanding presence. Just before sunset, we heard screaming from the streets below that caused us to run to the balcony overlooking the town square. Women were wailing uncontrollably while literally ripping off their shirts. Soon armed men with bandanas covering their faces appeared to steal vehicles to form roadblocks on the mountain roads leading to Pestel.

Apparently, Guy Phillipe had just been arrested in Miami on drug charges after being recently elected to the Haitian senate. At this moment, it did not matter if you considered Guy Phillipe to be a rebel, a drug fugitive, or a hero. The southern portion of Haiti belonged to him, and these were his people. He was instrumental in the removal of President Aristide and had recently engaged in a verbal battle with Haiti's interim president. His arrest mobilized southern Haiti, creating a militarized zone that was extremely unfriendly to Americans.

This incident was no surprise to a sovereign God. The woman running the guesthouse where we were staying turned out to be Guy Phillipe's wife. No one would have dared touch us while we were under her protection. We ended up sending our vehicle to Cafayier with one of our staff to wait out the turmoil. The rest of the team negotiated our escape on a motorboat. Under cover of darkness, we snuck out undetected. After clearing the most dangerous areas, we came ashore and found a tap tap going our way. I was relieved as we walked up the road leading to our compound. Once again, God had shown His sovereignty in a very clear manner.

And that is the singular point. Christ is sovereign; we are simply conduit vessels channeling His love, mercy, grace, and power to a hurting and dying world. When we fully embrace God's sovereignty, we are able to continue to serve under the most difficult of circumstances. What is number one must always remain number one. We are first and foremost messengers of the good news of the gospel. Never forget this because on your most difficult day you will remember that you still have a divine purpose and that our sovereign God is still on the throne. To Him be the honor and glory forever!

In His love,

Pastor D

My Dearest Macy and Mark,

Let me begin by expressing my deep sorrow, Macy, for the current chastisement you are receiving from your female peers regarding the slander being spread by some immature, childish male students. I fully agree that the whole situation is deplorable and hurtful. However, I would strongly suggest that you not take umbrage with these young men. Their innuendo is simply the means by which God is teaching you a valuable lesson early in your adventure with Him; we who serve the Lord and intend to lead others live in glass houses. Not just the windows are made of glass but the walls, ceilings, and floors as well. This is a lesson you both need to learn now.

Lesson 21: Glass Houses

Every great leader, pastor, prophet, and missionary will eventually come against the spirit of Jezebel. It is wrongly assumed that this spirit works solely on the sexual tension between men and women. Her aim is to discourage or destroy God's leaders.

Jezebel was the queen of Israel and wife to King Ahab. She interfered with Yahweh's exclusive right to be worshipped and was a proponent of the false god Baal. Her disregard for the common people, her defiance of the prophets Elijah and Elisha, and the ensuing internecine strife crippled Israel for a generation. Ten years after her husband was slain, Jehu, the newly anointed King of Israel, came to her palace. Expecting him, she adorned herself in a sultry, provocative manner and taunted him from her balcony. The king ordered her eunuchs to toss her from the balcony. When the king later ordered a royal burial, her body was found to have been mostly eaten by dogs as Elijah had foretold. Her attitude and actions caused her to become the archetype of the wicked woman.

Our battles are fought in the physical, spiritual, intellectual, and emotional realms. Accusation, whether unfounded or true, can be equally damaging. What do we do to protect ourselves, our relationships, our marriages, and our God-given positions? Some would propose that men and women should not be in discipleship together, which is a preposterous idea.

What should occur always is plausible deniability. That may have a derogatory sound to it, but let me assure you, that is what is needed. Never be alone with someone of the opposite sex. If it is a private conversation, then hold it in a public place where others can see you but not hear what is being said. It would be best to have your spouse or another trusted person present at all such encounters.

I have heard this story from several pastors, and although I cannot directly attest to its veracity, it does sound extremely plausible to me. I was told that Billy Graham would not enter his hotel room unless it was first checked for hidden women. That may seem crazy or even fanatical; nonetheless, I can assure you that the more kingdom influence God gives you, the more frequent and ferocious the enemy's attacks will be. In a war situation, the three people in the most danger within the platoon are usually noncombatants: the commanding officer, the radio operator, and the medic. Even though the rules of engagement protect these three individuals, they are taken out first because without them chaos ensues.

We can learn a lot about how to have proper relationships by looking at how Jesus organized His circles. In His inner circle were Peter, John, and James. The next circle included the rest of the disciples and arguably Mary Magdalene. The next circle included His friends such as Lazarus, Mary, and Martha. The next circle was composed of those He came to serve, followed by those who opposed Him. He trusted no one with His mission yet loved everyone fully.

This is a great lesson, one that will save you great pain if you heed it. In America love and trust are intertwined, but not so in the third world countries we serve. Time and time again, we've been emotionally wounded by those we loved and those with whom we served. We gave them jobs, food, treated their illnesses, entrusted them with responsibility within our ministry, discipled them, and mostly loved them. In response, they lied, stole, cheated, misrepresented, and maligned our efforts and reputations. God needed to teach us the very lesson that Jesus displayed in His relationships. They genuinely loved us and still acted in this manner. As Americans, we are viewed as something akin to dollar signs. They believe that if someone steals from us, then since we are rich, we will replace it. In Creole, there is no word for deceit simply because it is part of their culture.

An old missionary friend, since departed, told us the following stories that I have only recently gleaned the wisdom from.

- A Haitian man was walking along the beach and found a genie's bottle. He rubbed it, and the genie appeared and granted him anything his heart desired—with one stipulation. Whatever the man asked for he would give double to his neighbor. After some thought, the man asked the genie to make him blind in his left eye.

- A man hired a Haitian assistant to paint with him. He noticed that the man was painting from the bottom up and instructed him to paint from the top down, giving him all the reasons why this was the correct way to paint. They worked together for ten years until the painter retired and gave the man his business. Some time later, the man returned to Haiti, only to discover that his former assistant was painting from the bottom up. He questioned him, and the Haitian man replied, "This is how we do it in Haiti."

You will never be a native when you serve in a foreign mission, no matter how much you study the culture. When I first went to the mountains, God showed me little Josie, who became my poster child. Time and time again I made the arduous and dangerous trip to see her and all the mountain children. We paid for her school and her supplies each year. After five years, we decided to bring her on a short vacation to our home. As we prepared to bring her back to her home, my wife found that she had stuffed her bag with little treasures she had stolen over the course of the week. My wife removed the items and we laughed it off because she was only seven. When same thing happened some time later with older children and employees, the sting was more severe. Once we left Haiti, it was less than a week before our batteries, water cooler, and refrigerator were stolen. I estimate the value of cash and goods stolen over the course of our tenure to be well over twenty thousand dollars.

However, the most difficult incident for me involved a young Haitian woman. She told me that she had received bad street drugs, which had made her sick, and she needed to go to the hospital. The doctor informed me that she was pregnant and had botched the abortion attempt. I am vehemently opposed to abortion after seeing the traumatic effects it had on two close friends in my youth, not to mention the fact that I believe abortion to be outright murder. Therefore, now that I knew the truth, I had a decision to make: stick to my principles or help this young woman and show her the love and forgiveness that Christ has always shown me. It was not an easy decision and required some serious prayer, but I chose to help her. After some time, enlightenment from the Holy Spirit filled me. I now understood it was not about our mission or what we could accomplish; rather, it was simply about loving like Christ. We plant seeds and water them, nothing more, and nothing less. That is the lesson—love like Christ, and expect nothing in return.

In His love,

Pastor D

My Dearest Macy and Mark,

I am sure you remember that I taught science for over two decades, but I am uncertain if I ever explained that genetics and biochemistry were my concentration and passion. Today I would like to broach an extremely delicate subject, especially as it concerns the matter of sexual intimacy. As a missionary working with children, teens, and young adults, occasions will arise that necessitate your guidance of the young in matters of love and sexual intimacy. You may also find yourself fighting against sexual cultural norms in the adult population, which may further confuse and exacerbate youth's decision-making processes.

As a foreign unmarried couple, you will have your work cut out for you. You do have positional authority as missionaries and representatives of Jesus Christ, and I have no doubt that you will earn the right to speak into the lives of the young by demonstrating your great love for them. You may feel awkward and uncomfortable speaking about sexual matters; however, that does not negate your responsibility. I shied away from my responsibility to my children as a father, feeling that they knew about sexual relations, and I didn't want to make them uncomfortable with this type of discussion. We always had an open door policy concerning any topic they needed to discuss, which I felt was sufficient. I was wrong, simply because I did not arm them with the tools of knowledge necessary for young people to make decisions in such matters. I am convicted not to make the same mistake with you both.

Lesson 22: Speak Truth with Love

"Delicate"

If there is one temptation common to all humankind, it is sexual in nature. The standard position of the church has and always should be sexual abstinence outside of marriage. If that is all you tell a youth, then you may as well hand them a condom because you have pretty much guaranteed that they will proceed. There is a reason that I chose the song "Delicate" as an example for your lesson.

The song is brilliant, especially in how it portrays the subtle nuances that may lead us where we never thought we would go. Let us begin with the obvious: we are talking about an affair here. We are unsure if her object of desire is a married man or perhaps just a man of influence, but we can unequivocally state that this relationship is not out in the open— absolutely, positively the first warning sign of something you should not be doing. In fact, warning bells should be going off in your head and in your spirit.

The title is also layered with meanings. I would like to focus on four definitions of the word *delicate*. In today's vernacular, it may mean fragile, easily damaged; or it may mean so fine as to be barely perceptible, subtle. In the more archaic contexts, it may mean a source of pleasure, and the word *delicacy* is derived from it as well. If this were a straight-on assault, most Christians would run from it as Joseph did from Potiphar's wife.

I am going to assert something here that may cause you to take umbrage, but I would ask you to keep reading so that you may clearly grasp the ultimate point. It would be better to succumb to an all-out assault than to one that is delicate. What I mean by that is that a purely physical affair can be more easily overcome. I assure you that this is a cogent argument, and I am fully cognizant of the moral failings it entails. First and foremost, it is sin and breaks God's heart. If you are married, then it breaks the marriage covenant, and since you are fully one in the sight of God, you are defiling not only your own body but that of your spouse as well. If someone does not understand this, then that person really does not understand how God sees marriage. This also applies to someone in a position of power: if that person pushes for sexual relations from a subordinate, then they are abusing their power, whether that is their intent or not. To those who are single we should say; God is not trying to quell your fun. He loves you!

There is a biochemical change that occurs when you have sex with someone. Oxytocin is released in the body, simultaneously stimulating feelings of pleasure while inhibiting pain. The social salience of this chemical release is an approach/withdrawal response. This may lead to people finding themselves in precarious sexual relations. The easiest example of this mechanism can be seen by examining abusive relationships. If someone is dating platonically and they are struck by their partner, more than likely they will at least end the relationship; however, in a sexual relationship, they are much more likely to take the abuse and maybe even make excuses for their partner's behavior.

The release of oxytocin begins in a man during sexual arousal, while females need stimulation that is more direct. This is an important difference because it explains why the Bible instructs females to dress modestly. This was another mistake I made during my early days in missions. I allowed female members of my teams to dress in attire that was socially acceptable in Florida, which resulted in some fairly revealing attire. The halfhearted Christian side hug may seem superficial; however, a full body hug may also induce the unwanted release of oxytocin. Both of these seemingly harmless cases may elicit aggressive sexual behavior in certain males, especially in countries with different sexual norms.

Oxytocin is not all bad news for the Christian. Biologically men have a desire to breed with as many females as possible, which increases their DNA's chances of surviving; oxytocin release binds the man to the woman and induces him to stay with her and raise their children. This explains why a wife should not withhold sex from her husband. The other obvious reasons for abstaining from sexual relationships out of wedlock include unwanted pregnancies and STD transmission.

With that said, let us look at this song a little more closely because it clearly demonstrates escalation in a relationship. In the first stanza, we see what appears to be a harmless relationship, the realization that two people like each other ending in a drink. Most of us want to be liked or even loved by others. If you say or think that you cannot be tempted or that you have never been tempted, then in today's vernacular, "You lyin'." In the second stanza, they have transitioned to dating, and the battle is now being waged in the mind as she suggests all the fun things they can do. The repeating chorus is composed mostly of seemingly harmless questions that lead the battle from the mind to the bed in the next stanza. The song ends in what is now a full-blown relationship consisting of the mind, the physical, and now clearly the heart.

From my personal experience, I am going to propose to you that you can win the first two battles, but if you lose the battle of the heart, you may be in as bad a shape as if you had lost all three. I will also suggest that unfounded accusations can be equally damaging.

My advice to you both is not solely for those you serve and for those who serve under you, it applies to you as well. Discernment of intent is a slippery slope that may lead to a fall. You may look like Jesus to the natives, but you will most certainly also look like dollar signs. Loneliness is a powerful adversary, which demands satisfaction. Native females use their sexuality as a means to get men to care for them, and all the better if they get pregnant in the process, while men want to acquire power and to become successful. If you engage romantically with the natives, you are viewed as both predator and prey. I caution you to guard your heart concerning the indigenous you serve and not to become romantically entwined. I also would caution you to keep an appropriate distance from those you mentor and disciple and to always guard your heart in every relationship that you develop.

I leave you with a final story about a young woman I mentored when she was new to Haiti and education. She eventually started her own mission and grew it into a fully functional mission compound with the help of her church and supporters. It was quite successful and provided the children with daily Bible study, meals, and a safe place to play. She fell in love with a Haitian man, which resulted in their marriage. Once married, he stopped sexual relations with her and began sleeping with local Haitian women. He stole many assets from the ministry and eventually caused her to leave the field.

There is a season for everything. If it is His will and in His timing, you will be married; be patient! God chose my wife for me, and he could not have chosen a better woman. He has you both in the palm of His hand, covered in the blood of Christ and sealed in the Holy Spirit. I pray that you receive this advice in the spirit it was given and that it protects you in an hour of weakness. We are all flesh and blood; sinners each and every one. It is only the grace of God and our willingness to obey His command to go that allows us to carry on His work.

In His love,

Pastor D

My Dearest Macy and Mark,

I must admit that I am extremely conflicted concerning your call to minister to Syrian children in the refugee camps along the Turkish border. I am simultaneously both proud and deeply grieved as I weigh the merits against the dangers of such a call. The great need is blatantly obvious; however, as young attractive Christian missionaries from America, you could not be a more appealing target.

As we prepared for our first launch to Haiti, our pastor expressed fear over our station. We were perplexed because we were not afraid and fully embraced the protection that Psalm 91 offers. We viewed his fear as a lack of faith in God's mission and perhaps in God himself. As I pray over you now, I am beginning to understand our pastor's feelings. It is not fear of the worthiness of your call or your ability to carry it out; rather, it is the fear of losing you to a martyr's death or perhaps worse. Although fear is not of God, our love for you and desire for your safety most certainly is. As your mentor and spiritual father, your safety is of the utmost importance to me.

The sheer magnitude of your call demands that I express my feelings toward your impending mission. I fully believe that you are ready to handle the vigor and trauma of such a mission. My concern is founded on the urgency you will feel as you proceed with the benignities born of your selfless devotion. As I reflect on my time in the third world, the outreaches I treasured so dearly fade into an evanescent memory. The tangible realities indelibly seared into my memories are the times I simply held a child or played with them. It is those times of just being and not doing that matter most. Nothing will destroy a missionary faster than assuming the whole weight of His call. You are not God, and as such, you are only responsible for what He asks of you. Live, laugh, and love every day, and you will flourish

Lesson 23: Be Present in the Moment

> I must be without remorse or regrets as I am
> Without excuse; for from the instant of my
> Upsurge into being, I carry the weight of the
> World by myself alone without help, engaged
> In a world for which I bear the whole
> Responsibility without being able, whatever I
> Do, to tear myself away from this
> Responsibility for an instant.
>
> —Jean-Paul Sartre

Sartre was utterly wrong; it is simply about love. God gives you a season, and when that season ends, it is simply about how much of His love you poured out to those He has given you. You cannot make it last a moment longer; therefore, you must relish every second He gives you.

My greatest regret from my first decade serving in missions is that I never learned this lesson until the season had passed. My heart yearns as tears still flow for the precious moments spent with children and comrades while in His service.

I have no earth-shattering revelations to share; only brief moments of love and joy. Many of the children's names already elude me, as our days together quickly vanish into years apart. Some of my most precious memories are sitting in the hall at our first compound playing games on my phone with the children. I loved finding a place in the shade to sit on a hot afternoon because inevitably within five minutes I would be literally covered with children.

There are so many great memories of taking the children to the beach both at Locul and at Taino or watching as my little Valentina or Josie's face would light up, breaking into a huge smiles when they saw me. Holding orphans so desperate for love that they would never ask to get down was another favorite pastime of mine. The memory of walking up the hill to feed the malnourished twins and neighboring children and then sitting in the dirt while they ate brings me great joy. Hearing my name yelled out nearly everywhere we went fills my heart with love. The countless drives through the countryside, watching as the children would run toward us in hopes of candy, food, or a simple "we love you," were richly rewarding. I loved watching the children play after the feeding program at Project Eden, and I could always get a laugh when a child scaled the wall of our compound in the early morning hours yelling my name. My response was always the same: *Pastor D pa la* (Pastor D is not here), which always yielded audible laughter. I cherish the good times and laughs shared with our five little Haitian daughters and their caregivers.

Perhaps my favorite memories come from watching those young adults like you as they fell in love with the Haitian country, their children, and the sheer joy of serving the neediest among us. Do not miss a second of every precious moment of love with those who you have been sent to serve.

In His love,

Pastor D

My Dearest Macy and Mark,

Well, here you are, beginning your last semester. It seems the time has flown by, though perhaps not for you, as I can tell that your yearning toward graduation and mission commission is peaking. We still have much work to accomplish between now and then. It is my fervent belief that you are now prepared for what I am about to share with you. I have waited for such a time as this, not wishing to scare or deter you from your call; nonetheless, you must be fully prepared for what lies in wait for you.

The world we do not see is exponentially more real than the one that lies before us. There is a war raging in the heavens for the souls that populate humankind. You have chosen to put on God's armor and fight the horrors of the demonic horde. You must be fully cognizant of what that entails before you draw His sword.

The greatest lie ever perpetrated by Satan was convincing most people that he does not exist. Let me assure you, this is not some melancholy tale preached from the pulpit to cajole parishioners to acquiesce into willful submission and obedience. It is a very real battle over the sanctity of life and for the final resting place of humanity's souls. Each battle will be fought over faith, hope, and love. It is fought in the trenches, and it is a knife fight in which you must not hesitate to cut the enemies' throats one by one. It is messy, and before its end, you will be battered and weary.

At times, it may seem you are fighting against the very flesh and blood beings that you are trying to save. Let me assure you of the illusory nature of those feelings. It is God's desire not to lose any of His children, no matter how evil or callous they may seem to our mortal eyes. The "us against them" mentality many Christians have adopted is in reality a device of the enemy. It really is "love the sinners, and give your life for the sinners." We all sin, and we all need a loving Savior who gave His life to blot out our sins once and for all. Only we as humans differentiate between "levels" of sin. Sin is sin in God's eyes. Love is your weapon that brings the faith and hope back to the lost. No matter the horror, never forget that you are the salt and life needed in a hurting and dying world.

Lesson 24: God Knows

Angels and Demons

> We came upon a small Afghani town where the people were starving. They looked upon us with suspicion and mistrust, but soon welcomed us as we set them up with food, clean water, and friendly smiles. It was not long until we said our goodbyes as our mission called for us to proceed to the next town. Upon our return, we found the town decimated, every man, woman, and child had been beheaded. Their heads displayed on stakes as a message to us and to all Afghani's that would receive aid from us.
>
> —quote from a good friend

Certain things have happened in my life that I simply do not share with people. The world might describe many of these things as supernatural, yet they are simply spiritual manifestations. As I told you already, an angel came to me while I was in bed, aged eleven. Terrified, I covered my head with a blanket while he ministered to me. After a few minutes, I was no longer scared and pulled the blanket away to find the angel gone. At fifteen, I was praying, and the Holy Spirit was so strong upon me that all I could do was weep in His presence.

When I was a young Christian, pure of heart and full of zeal, God granted me the gift to see briefly into the spiritual world. It terrified me so that I begged him to remove my spiritual sight, which He granted immediately. The problem, though, was that my not seeing angels and demons did not make them less real.

As a missionary, one is subject to a relentless onslaught of attacks taking various forms. Some attacks are flagrant and easily detectable, while others manifest themselves in more subtle ways. You must be able to control your mind, or you will lose the battle before you even begin to fight. There are curses, voodoo, or otherwise destructive devices that may be cast your way—not to mention people who would directly pray against you. The most difficult for me is sleep. I do not control the sleep dimension, and what I can only describe as night terrors and assaults on my very being occur all too frequently. Eventually, lack of peace may lead you to strange behavior or purposely avoiding trauma. If trauma is left unchecked and unhealed by God, PTSD is a very real possibility. Prayer and conviction of my mission are the only two things that have ever helped me.

You may not believe me now, but when you are faced one on one with the demonic in the field, I pray you call on the power of God, the Holy Spirit, and the blood of Jesus to help you. The demonic might confront you while like looking in a tent and finding the red glowing eyes of a demon staring back at you, or at church when a demon attacks a teenage boy in the middle of service and you are the only spiritual authority there to cast it out. It could be a demonic stare while God is prophesying through you, from someone who speaks no English but understands every word. It may be even more bizarre like a voodoo priestess slithering up a tree like a snake. You may be called to boldness walking into a voodoo temple to rescue a sick girl from an altar. Even though those were my experiences, I urge you, no matter what comes against you, to remember that our God is more than enough.

The physical manifestations can also be daunting. I have suffered through yet by the grace of God endured the Zika and chikungunya viruses. I have had a spider bite me that was carrying necrotizing strep A bacteria, which attempted to eat my leg to the bone. I battled through a year of on-and-off dysentery, outlasted a fever of unknown origin that lasted for six weeks, and overcame a potentially lethal bacterium causing my teeth to break one by one while placing me at high risk for a heart attack, stroke, and kidney failure. I say all this not to scare you but to remind you that I am fine. We could not do what we do without the assurance of and belief in Psalm 91. If God is for you, then surely nothing can be against you.

I believe that you are much like me, and therefore your most difficult battles will be fought in the emotional realms when you are confronted with unfathomable horror. Walking over the hundred thousand–plus bodies buried in Haiti's mass grave leaves one reticently silent. The sanctity of life becomes a very real issue, one that is all too easily blurred when we are embroiled in matters of life and death within the third world. The days of being a stargazer abruptly and brutally end when you hold a dying child, and she looks into your eyes as if you are her last hope for life.

Driving is no less deleterious as you cover more ground in a shorter time. We watched in helpless shock as a woman was run over by several vehicles before someone got out and rolled her lifeless body into the gutter with the mud and garbage. On another occasion, we watched as a crowd with clubs continuously pummeled a man's lifeless body or as someone was being engulfed with tires just before they set him on fire. Police leave examples of the bodies of bullet-ridden gang members on the street as witnessed by a team of my students. The stench of trucks filled with debris and littered with decaying bodies reaches you long before the trucks ever appear. The memory of cries from the lawless streets of Cité Soleil to the remote mountain villages of starving children too weak to walk fill your restless dreams causing tears to run down your cheeks soaking your pillow.

Through the entirety of this, God has not been absent or silent. I have seen with my own eyes the dead raised, the blind made to see, and the crippled walk. I have prayed for babies with virtually no chance of survival, and when I returned, they were thriving. Many lost souls have come to Him and many more have begun the process of discipleship. My advice to you both is to pray without ceasing and do not be afraid. You sit in the Father's hand, covered by the blood of Christ, and sealed in the Holy Spirit.

You cannot save, feed, heal, or clothe anyone on your own, but God can do all this and much more. I will leave you with this one story from a missionary mentor and friend. A voodoo priest cursed him, saying that he would die by morning. The missionary laughed and told him that God and the blood of the Lamb protected him. The next morning Haitians came running up to him and told him that the voodoo priest had died overnight. The little god of this world does not compare to the God you serve. Never forget this lesson!

In His love,

Pastor D

My Dearest Macy and Mark,

I would like to begin today's lesson with a few words about trust. To be successful missionaries you must enjoy a modicum of trust. Your trust in God must be absolute. He is your lifeblood in countless ways when you are serving in the foreign mission field. Without unfettered trust in God, you are doomed to fail. You must also trust each other above all other humans.

The trust of everyone else is a matter for you and the Holy Spirit to work out. Disciples, mentees, and other missionaries can usually be counted on to be fairly trustworthy in matters of ministry. Do not share intimate struggles with them! To a lesser degree, you need to trust your employees, at least with their assigned duties. The two of you should solely manage anything valuable. I am not only speaking of material assets and money, but also your struggles, hopes, fears, and faith.

If any chink in your armor shows, it will be used against you. In public, you must present yourself as the epitome of righteousness. This is not a façade, but rather a representation of whom you serve. In the States, it is perfectly acceptable for a pastor to show his frailty and shortcomings. It may help connect him with his struggling congregation and may prevent them from placing him on a pedestal. However, you will not be in the United States; instead, you will be under constant scrutiny by those who would destroy what God is accomplishing through you.

My final thought concerning trust has to do with those whom you chose to invite to serve with you. Once you establish yourselves, you may want to host or lead short-term mission teams. After a year or more, you may also want to disciple an intern as well. You have the final word on who serves with you. It is perfectly acceptable to say no. You are responsible for those under you, so be careful. When we accepted Neria as an intern, she was someone we had experience with. We had met her while in Bible college and we were part of a team in Mexico with her. We also led her and her mission team in Haiti and were able to bring them to experience the mountain ministry. She and her team served during the largest clinic we ever held, and they did an amazing job.

The point is this: she was not a stranger. We had a good feeling about her and knew her capabilities. On the other hand, I once had a team member who was too old, and even though I lightened the itinerary, it was too much for her. I had another team member tell me he was solely a tourist and was only going to observe. Make your expectations clear before your teams arrive. If someone becomes a problem with no resolution, put that person on a plane, and send them home. Send detailed instructions to potential visitors. Include release forms, permission slips for minors, and a list of medications or vaccinations needed, along with packing guidelines and dress codes. Prepare them for what they will be doing and experiencing. You must teach them about the local customs. They must also be able to differentiate between ethics and morals when serving in another culture.

Lesson 25: Decide Whom You Will Serve

Ethics and Morals

Every day when you wake in the third world, you will have new and difficult choices to make. They are a big part of the job. Choosing what type of missionary you will be determines the range of choices available to you. You are not ignorant of the fact that, whatever choices you make, there will be both advantages and disadvantages.

Joining a community of American missionaries solves many issues such as loneliness and the feelings of isolation that most certainly will develop over time. It provides some normalcy and familiarity as you adjust to a new culture. It may even produce wisdom because in theory you will have many experienced counselors. Conversely, assimilation into the culture then becomes extremely difficult. The risk is that one leaves the security of their compound walls simply to do a job and return. Taking advice from other missionaries may also become problematic, as their advice is based upon their experiences and therefore may be jaded and certainly will contain bias. Personally, this was not the right fit for us; neither do I feel that it is the right fit for you.

We began our full-time ministry with an organization. The greatest advantage was the financial support it offered in the way of monetary funds, vehicles, and all the other supplies needed to carry out ministry in the field. This is a very personal decision and one we discovered was not right for us either. We began our short-term ministry with this organization as partners, which worked very well. When we committed to full-time ministry, they trained us and provided for us during that season. We will always be very grateful, and we love them to this day.

However, working as missionaries for an organization has many drawbacks as well. Most missionaries' purpose is to serve God and therefore commune regularly with Him. The fundamental idea is that direction is provided from the ultimate source. When missionaries work for an organization, they become employees and as such are expected to follow the organization's agenda regardless of their call and direction from the Holy Spirit. It plainly becomes a job. Ultimately, this was not a good fit for us either.

Living among the people is the best choice whenever possible. There are some serious concerns regarding safety, privacy, theft, and vandalism, all of which we had to deal with. In our case, it was still the most advantageous. We learned the language and the customs much faster and built much deeper relationships with many more people, especially the children. Although we had walls, they served to protect the children rather than keep the indigenous out. Amusingly, we found that almost all the children were capable of climbing the eight-foot wall surrounding our compound home. We increased the number of children who were fed daily from sixty to one hundred, and each of them attended a children's church service before the feeding. The relationships we built with the older teens allowed us to keep abreast of what was occurring in the area. I ended up providing medical care for about one thousand people; if need be I would hike to their homes to minister physically and spiritually to them.

We were able to provide educational funds for about fifty children all from the grace of God. It taught us to trust in Him simply because we had no other choice. On several occasions, we did not know how we would pay for what God asked us to do. In each case, just before we were about to lose hope, people we had never met contacted us and donated generously. In each instance, it was exactly what we needed. We learned that God is seldom early; however, He is never late. Because we lived with virtually no privacy, especially after we took in our five girls, we chose Friday as our day off. This was a necessity for us to delay field burnout.

Typically, we went to a little French bistro on Taino beach where we would swim, relax, play some cards, and enjoy a bite to eat. It was still Haiti though! On one occasion, we were sitting on chairs by the sand and a couple of natives decided that they were going to have sex not fifty feet from us. Needless to say, we were surprised, yet not shocked. This leads me to explain why I chose this topic for your instruction. We were also able to escape the rigors of the daily grind by taking a weekend at Decameron, a five-star resort in the north of Haiti. Although this was needed and very relaxing, we paid dearly for it, as much of the theft occurred while we were away.

Every culture has its own set of ethics and morals. Many aspects of foreign culture offend our Western sense of propriety, at least superficially. Our immense obsession concerning sexual matters is surpassed only by our incessant need to obscure it. We espouse modesty and chastity while simultaneously being bombarded with media and advertisements loaded with sexual innuendo. Little girls are made to look like twenty-year-olds, and young women are barely clad enough to keep the censors placated. Meanwhile, the rest of the world finds humor in our preoccupation with modesty while presenting an obvious predilection toward nudity so long as it is hidden.

Haiti's mores were equally difficult to understand. Nudity in public was perfectly acceptable under certain circumstances such as bathing and swimming. One of my greatest concerns was the vulnerability of the children bathing at our community water station not fifty feet from the major highway in southern Haiti. This offended my ethical sense; however, I was perfectly all right with the same nudity at the beaches. This was a double standard that sprang from my upbringing in the American culture. It was not morally wrong, just concerning to my personal standards.

This is not to say that there are not moral failings within the culture. Haiti was the first free black Caribbean nation. From this achievement stems a great sense of pride, which unfortunately spills into many other prideful areas. Children sold by their parents as restaveks (domestic, labor, and sexual child slaves) is a fairly common practice, although Haitians vehemently deny it exists. Marital affairs were also very common, even among the moral leaders within the society.

Here lay much of the moral dilemma. Preaching chastity to the unmarried and fidelity to the married actually went against the social norms of the society. The solution involved much time and prayer. We are never to stop preaching biblical commands and values; however, we are also never to judge or stop providing love and mercy.

During our last year in Haiti, a man was having an affair with a much younger girl still living under her parents' roof. She may have actually been under the age of eighteen. He was married and had a couple of children still at home. He came to me for advice, as his girlfriend had become pregnant and wanted to abort the child. His request was money for the abortion, which he thought would solve the problem, allowing him to continue the immoral affair, hiding it from both her parents and his wife. This man had undergone discipleship training and should have been able to see the moral failings in his request. Nevertheless, my response and offer surprised him. I would give his girlfriend the money necessary to have the child but not to abort it. This was an example of the moral superseding the ethical. In this case, the unborn child was the innocent who needed protection.

We were once in a mildly heated discussion that ensued because I had half-jokingly suggested that we get a helicopter and fly as many starving children out of the mountains as we could. One pastor began to explain how unethical my comments were, when another pastor chimed in, stating that we should never worry about the ethical when the moral is at stake. I never forgot this conversation, and that pastor became a great friend and adviser to us, literally saving our marriage at one juncture and providing necessary counsel and advice during times of despair while we served in the field.

The moral rose above the ethical many times in our decision making process. It allowed us to take nine malnourished children out of the mountains for care even though we did not know how the bills would be paid for. The moral allowed us to pay for selected children that God placed on our hearts to be educated or receive special medical attention. It was what allowed us to take in five little girls and improve their condition. Most importantly, it allowed us to love unconditionally and without judgment even when behaviors offended our sense of ethical behavior.

This is a lesson I pray God instills in you both. We are all wretched sinners before the pure and spotless Lamb of God. It is only because of His love, mercy, grace, and forgiveness that we are enabled to serve His children. It was once said of me that my responses to situational circumstances were unpredictable. This is most certainly untrue. I will always err on the side of mercy and grace, putting the needs of God's little ones above everything else. As you pray about your living arrangements in the field, remember: this attitude makes for very poor employees and very good missionaries.

In His love,
Pastor D

My Dearest Macy and Mark,

As a missionary called to serve in the third world, there are important yet practical lessons we need to learn. They are counterintuitive lessons, which run against our very nature. As a leader, we are called to protect, disciple, and guide our teams with the utmost importance being given to their safety. My question to you both then becomes, if you go down as the leader, then who will lead?

Lesson 26: Protect Yourselves

Although this advice may seem a little simplistic and pragmatic, I can assure you of its necessity. Both my wife and I are highly parental figures, and as such, we guide our mission's teams as if they were our children. You both are my spiritual children and as such my advice to you is of that of a loving father. My job is to not solely instruct you but also to protect you whenever circumstances deem it necessary.

Physical protection may be found in two forms, both of which may be aided by wisdom. Take no unnecessary risks with yourself or your teams. I cannot overstress the value of educating and training your native staff to watch over your mission teams—and you, for that matter. In a public venue such as a restaurant, always sit with your back against a wall with a full view of your environment. At outreaches, back the vehicles in for a quick exit, and surround your mission team with native staff. When hiking in remote areas make sure that your staff is both leading and following.

Team members should never be allowed to wander off by themselves; in fact, it is a good policy to use the buddy system so that everyone can be accounted for at all times, including trips for showers and restrooms. If no one else is available, then you must stand watch within shouting distance. Some team members may be dealing with fear and others may not possess the wisdom to be careful. Your teams may misconstrue your actions, so informing them in advance about the safety precautions should put everyone at ease.

Be aware that, with all that I have suggested, you still may encounter problems. On one trip, I experienced both extremes of this scenario. One of my team members, a teenaged female, was having intestinal distress, and a senior female member did not want me with them. I resolved the issue by standing far enough away so that there was a modicum of privacy, yet close enough to get there quickly if an intruder should present himself.

The other issue was also a restroom issue, as we needed vehicle repair in the middle of Port-au-Prince. We were there for several hours, and Kefira and Maya needed the restroom. A man we did not know offered to take them, and my driver refused to go; therefore, I jumped out and escorted them.

Occasionally you will receive a team member you do not know, who will not respect your authority. As I have already mentioned, once you have exhausted every method of instruction and warning, if such a member is a danger to the team, send them home! If the person is only a danger to himself or herself, then let the Holy Spirit guide you. We had a middle-aged man that our Haitian team referred to as *"blan foo,"* which translates as white fool. He refused instruction and continually wandered off by himself in areas that could have resulted in his kidnapping or death. Unfortunately, we were deep within a remote mountain area, and sending him home was not a possibility. As a result, we needed to assign him an adult babysitter, which put a strain on the team because we did not have any extra staff along.

Concerns about safety for yourselves and others call for wisdom, which God has promised to give you freely if you simply ask.

In His love,

Pastor D

My Dearest Macy and Mark,

Have either of you ever heard the term *Coram Deo*? It is a Latin phrase, which loosely translated means that we who serve God live in His presence, under His authority, and for His honor and glory. Before you hit the ground and are able to minister to the Syrian refugee children, you must know Jesus. Stop laughing! This may seem like a childishly naïve statement; however, I can assure you of its importance. I am not writing out of any concern or doubt about your salvation or love of Christ. There is a marked difference between knowing who Jesus is and accepting Him as your Savior, even serving Him full-time, and knowing who He really is—His character, His grace, His mercy, and His love.

Lesson 27: Coram Deo

We really did not understand who Christ was fully while we were engaged in short-term missions. There was not a real and pressing need to know Him fully. We operated under His protection and followed the lead and power of the Holy Spirit. We who serve are fully capable of this under short-term conditions; the pressure of full time foreign missions requires a much deeper relationship with Jesus. He is literally your life source, and you are literally His mouth, hands, and feet. When people look at you, they see Jesus. I have already shared with you the story of the little boy who saw me and yelled out "Jesus," pointing to me. The tears I wept as I pulled over were not tears of regretful unworthiness; they were the beginning of my maturation and realization of who the real Jesus is.

I have shared that we were robbed, threatened, maligned, lied to, lied about, and deceived on a daily basis. These events were allowed to happen not to hurt us but so that we might fully know who Jesus is. Think for a moment about Jesus's life here on Earth. Do any of the things I have mentioned even come close to what He endured for our forgiveness and eternal salvation? When you really know Jesus, there is nothing you cannot forgive.

Remember, real forgiveness brings us back to the moment just before the offense occurred, with no lingering memory or pain. In 2 Samuel 6, we see that when King David successfully brought the Ark of the Covenant to Jerusalem, he sacrificed a bull after six steps. Imagine looking backward as the Ark moved; the only thing visible on the path would have been blood. That is what the blood of Christ accomplished for us and how we must learn to forgive in the same manner. When the Father looks back at our lives, it is only the blood of Christ He sees.

There is a reason for every bad action; we do not judge those reasons or even need to know them; we need only show mercy and grace. We bring hope through the knowledge of who Jesus is and discipleship through His instruction to us. There will be times that you will need to correct behavior and perhaps even false doctrine, but always do it with a gentle spirit of love. Jesus is the reason; we bring His light and love to the darkness of this world—that is the mission, pure and simple. Please pray for a deeper intimacy with Jesus; He is your only hope and salvation once you enter the field.

In His love,

Pastor D

My Dearest Macy and Mark

As you begin your last two months of training, I feel it apropos to discuss endings. Seasons change, and as joyful or painful as that might be, we must change with them, but not before taking the prescribed time for God to minister to us. When we returned to the United States, we experienced what I would call reverse culture shock. The sheer magnitude of the carnality of American culture was overwhelming. This was coupled with feelings of great loss and guilt over abandoning the children we love and cared for.

Our transition back into American culture took a great deal of time and in many respects is still ongoing. I believe that my place is in the field, ministering to suffering and neglected children. In this season of returning to short-term missions, I simply count the days until I may serve in the foreign mission fields again. Once you have engaged in your creation purpose, everything else seems trivial and unsatisfying. We must learn to mourn our losses in a healthy manner, allowing God to be our healer. "'For I know the plans I have for you,' declares the Lord, 'plans to prosper you and not to harm you, plans to give you hope and a future'" (Jeremiah 29:11). These words to live by can be a healing balm as our seasons change. The following account is my first interactions with Master's Commission students such as you. I pray the account inspires you.

Lesson 28: Seasons Change

Rise

I thought myself healed and ready to begin our mission work again; I was woefully mistaken. The mission trip into Castillo del Rey in El Salvador was uneventful and quite pleasurable as compared to mission trips into Haiti. It did not take long to recognize the many differences between the countries; especially how Americanized the cities were, including perhaps every major fast food chain. I wondered how I would react to a culture not in the throes of imminent crisis.

We arrived just in time to be part of a four-day Miracle Crusade. I have to admit I was not excited. I felt that I could go to church in the States and therefore wanted to get my hands dirty serving the needy children. God, however, had other plans! This trip was not about me serving; rather, it was about God healing me in ways that I had never fathomed. Castillo del Rey is a large and very nice facility. I was given my own little apartment that was very comfortable and quaint. The food was good, and I was seldom hungry. We were paired with a team from Michigan and assigned four incredible and lovable Master's Commission students, including our interpreter, Ari, to aid us and guide us through our stay.

The first night of the crusade was held in the camp gym. A few people from the area attended, as well as the Master's Commission students from El Salvador and Nicaragua, who made up the bulk of the audience. Everything was preached in Spanish, and although I had held my own in the car, I was tired and unable to follow most of what was said. The service ended with an altar call for any who needed healing. I went up to pray behind the sick, but did not fully engage myself. As things were wrapping up, a few people were still being prayed for. I felt the tug of the Holy Spirit urging me to ask for prayer for my knee, which had never healed in the nine months since I had returned from Haiti. I asked the pastor to pray for me, and before he did, he questioned me. I told him about all the guilt I was feeling about leaving the children in Haiti. I did not intend to share this until it just came spilling out. He told me that sickness and injury often had internal components. He made me release the guilt and repeat that there is no condemnation in Christ Jesus in my prayer. He then prayed for my knee. He asked how it felt on a scale of one to ten after he prayed, with ten being the healthy state. I responded with seven, since it did seem better. He prayed again, and this time it popped. Over the next few days, it continued to get better; at times, I had to think about which knee was hurt.

The next day we had the morning free to look around. It was a beautiful sunrise and I began to feel a peace that had eluded me for a very long time. I went over and watched the monkeys playing for a while before heading up the hill to breakfast.

Afterward I toured the campus and was very impressed with the depot, sewing room, and Bible college. The depot is huge and filled with everything from shoes and clothes to food. The supplies are stored there simply because there are not enough hands to sort, process, and deliver the items to those in need. While the women sewed, I went back to my room. I soon heard music and emerged into the middle of a praise concert and message directed to teens from nearby schools. It was simply joyous watching the students engage and give God praise.

The highlight of the day, the week, and maybe the year was the evening crusade held at a small church in Candelaria. We arrived very early, which gave us an opportunity to meet some of the students. I was most impressed by two third-year students named Zahara and Naaman. Zahara's fourth year will be spent in Madrid where there is only one active children's ministry for two hundred churches. She will be traveling from church to church, training leaders and starting children's ministries all year.

The praise and worship were amazing, followed by a strong message that I was actually able to follow. There were many more healings in this service, and I thought it went well. However, as I was preparing to leave, the Holy Spirit had other ideas. The Spirit fell so strongly that people were melting in His presence. Weeping, passing out in the Spirit, and an intense need to exalt and praise God permeated the room as those of us still capable laid hands on and prayed for as many as we could. It was amazing and awesome all at one time.

What stands out most to me is the tenacity of the Master's Commission students when it comes to praying for healing. They do not even entertain the notion that God will not show up in a big way. By faith, they pray until God answers. Not for five or ten minutes or even an hour; they literally pray until God answers or the pastor shuts off the lights and asks them to leave. I pray God give you both such tenacity, zeal, and fervor for the sick and hurting.

The crusade then moved to a large tent church for the weekend services. I love outdoor services and the ability to worship surrounded by the beauty of His creation. The service ended with the pastors and Master's Commission students praying for the sick and injured. Two of the many miracles we witnessed remain engraved in my memory. A blind woman received her sight, and a man who had not walked in twelve years got up from his wheelchair and took thirty steps. I was in awe of God's power and majesty.

While the Master's Commission students prayed, I walked behind those receiving praying in the Spirit and laying hands on the sick as the Holy Spirit led. My head snapped up as I heard one of the students praying in English. Our eyes met as I mouthed the question, "American"? She nodded and later found me at the conclusion of service. She was a first-year student named Bracha and a college soccer player back in the States. I felt an immediate connection to her and firmly believed that I should somehow help her.

Before leaving El Salvador, I connected with about a dozen or so Master's Commission students on Facebook. That number has since grown fivefold. Bracha began corresponding with me as she was spiraling down a path of uneasiness concerning her call in El Salvador. Shortly God answered her prayers and called her to minister in Zambia, Africa, that coming summer. By the grace of God, we were able to assist her financially as well as providing a great deal of discipleship about ministering in the third world. She is currently planning another missionary internship in the Dominican Republic this summer.

It is a blessing to watch God's process raising up future leaders and missionaries. It was through this experience that God revealed to me that I did not need to be physically present to disciple and guide someone. The results of this revelation are these letters to you. As God shuts one door, He will open another once you are ready to walk through it.

In His love,

Pastor D

My Dearest Macy and Mark,

Wow, graduation is next month. Your excitement must be peaking, as well as your eager expectation to get into the field and begin your call at your chosen station. I feel compelled to make sure that this anticipation is directed in a positive manner so that it may reassure you and assist you in your last minute preparations. I have enlisted the aid of Pastor M and other young adults who have served alongside us to help encourage and prepare you. My concern is that my instruction is based solely on my mindset, and so I may have missed important components in your preparation. Pastor M has provided very practical advice, which will serve you well as you transition into the field. All the testimonies are from young disciples or other youth sharing their desire to serve, including any doubts they may have had before their first mission.

Lesson 29: You Have Purpose

As iron sharpens iron,
so one person sharpens another. (Proverbs 27:17)

Without counsel, plans go awry,
but in the multitude of counselors they are established.
(Proverbs 15:22)

You are both a big part of the Lord's army. Your greatest weapon and ultimate purpose is to share the hope you have in Jesus. You will never save anyone by your own volition; rather, it will be by the saving grace and mercy of our Lord Jesus and the power of the Holy Spirit. No matter the outcome, you will be forever changed simply because you said yes when called upon. I pray the following testimonies from young adults who have served alongside us inspire you.

> My heart drives my need to serve others. I honestly do not know what else I see myself doing in life, and I have this burning passion to consistently help and aid people in life. There is something about seeing others have victory in life and to come alongside them and cheer them on that makes my heart elated and gives me a peace from God. Before my first mission, my main concern was the fundraising—how and when God would provide. However, it was always in the unknown that God immeasurably met my financial needs for missions.
>
> —Bracha

I have this desire to be like Jesus. He was all about meeting the needs of the people He loved. He was literally sent to us to meet our needs. Knowing how it feels when you are in need drives me to help those who are too. I was pretty young the first time I ever went on a mission trip, but I remember thinking I was too young. Even when I was older, I struggled to see that I was even enough to make a difference in someone's life. Almost like the world was too good for me to help.

—Adar

Before I joined Achievers, I never really did community service, but I was active in my church. When I learned more about the club, it was not a question if I should join or not; something in me told me I had to join. I knew that it was bigger than I was. From that point on, I never looked back. I did not have any concerns before my first mission trip. I was actually confused as to why my family was so concerned. I was not nervous; I was ready to dive in. There was not a negative thought in my mind. I knew that God would protect me while I was doing His work.

—Maya

Serving was always my calling, but I didn't know it until I joined Achievers. Now helping is not just for the needy; it is for anyone and everyone who needs help, whether it is an ear to listen or a food donation. This club helped open my eyes and heart to endless opportunities of helping others and what it truly means. My life is forever changed. Thank you for all that you do and continue to do.

—Miryam

When I began the Achievers, I knew what needed to be done. The moment I landed in Haiti my life changed instantly, as did my perspective. I am forever a different person since I started. My motivation was knowing we are giving these people hope. Thank you for allowing me on this journey with you. I had no concerns before my first mission; I was ready from day one.

—Abarrane

After I'd been saved for four months, God made me understand that I had a purpose, and He made me feel loved like no one had before. Once He called me to become a missionary, I felt that I needed to bring that same love to others and that I needed to show the same mercy and love that He has shown me. When I am among them and see what is happening to them, I just want to help them, but sometimes it is not as easy as I would like. The main concern I had after my first mission trip was that I might not be able to return to the same place, and if I did, I would not be able to find the same people. I want to help people become leaders; that way, if I cannot return to a place, they can.

—Ari

Around the time I joined, my family was going through a tough time. It was something we had no control over and that was never going to change. During that time, I wanted to find light, which I did when I joined Achievers. After several events, I realized that every single one of us goes through something. I felt like I always have something to spare that someone else lacks, whether that is physically, mentally, or emotionally. In return, I felt like the experiences in helping others filled some lacking categories of mine. My main concern before my first mission was whether I was ready to endure what I was going to experience. Due to things that were said and showed to us in order to mentally prepare us, I started to question how much help I was really going to be. I will forever be thankful for being a part of the Achievers; it made me the person I am today.

—Hannah

I first heard of the Achievers at the last minute because my best friend was going on a mission trip and she told me what she'd be doing. Something screamed at me that I wanted to be on this trip. I was desperately trying to get approvals and money together to be able to experience it. My trip gave me a sense of purpose. It helped me discover myself after a bad breakup and showed me how much others suffer. I still remember all the little faces we served. My biggest concern was safety and the food I would eat, since I am so fussy. However, I felt safe in the compound and with the staff, and the food was amazing. I'm grateful for the opportunity to have served with you guys and really get a deeper sense of who I am.

—Avivit

Our advice on packing is simple; only bring what is necessary, and do not bring anything that is irreplaceable. You will need a variety of clothing, since winter temperatures can be below freezing, and summertime highs average above one hundred degrees. It is very arid and therefore the ample and incessant dust will be a challenge.

You should be aware of the utility situation. We carried water for our first two months and lived on generator power for most of our time in Haiti. The water may not be potable; if that is the case, boiling it for ten minutes or adding two drops of bleach to each liter of water should do the trick. You should always carry water with you, and having a couple of life straws in your daypacks is a good idea.

You will also want to know if there is Wi-Fi available. At times, this will be your only lifeline to the outside world. Your phones may or may not work; your Spot device will also be suspect at times. When using the Spot, make sure you are outside with the device pointing upward. Once you have pressed the SOS button, keep it on for at least thirty minutes. I cannot overstress the need for you to follow this advice; it may save your lives.

I recommend you ship an American four-wheel drive SUV, filled with all your necessities. We brought an American propane grill with us that turned out to be really beneficial. The last thing you will feel like doing after a full day of outreach is cooking in an oppressively hot kitchen.

You will need adapters to allow your American electronics to work with DC current. I suggest you buy an assortment so that you are covered no matter which country you are in. If you are blessed with an A/C, it probably will only cool the bedroom, and you will most likely only be able to run it while you sleep. Buy the A/C in the States, and load it in your SUV. Our last year in Haiti we had no A/C, which caused us to lie awake for hours, finally falling asleep in a pool of sweat. It left us weak, with impaired judgment, and vulnerable to disease and sickness. Ultimately, I believe it contributed to our exodus.

Before you leave, you will need inoculations for Hepatitis A and B, rabies, and typhoid. Do not ignore the typhoid vaccine, since you will eventually eat contaminated food. Although malaria and cholera are not too common in this region, I would still highly recommend a good supply of ciprofloxacin and Malarone.

I understand that you are anxious to get to your post; however, I would also recommend MMI's missionary medical course. You may be the only people with medical training in your area, and as such, you must be able to meet the people's needs. We held a dozen semiannual clinics across southern Haiti as well as being the sole medical source for about a thousand people surrounding our compound. There is a course starting just after your graduation in western North Carolina. You will be living in a militarized zone. This may necessitate treatment of war-related injuries as well. Let us know if you need financial assistance so that we may donate and help you fundraise support for your tuition.

I realize that your financial commitments cover your cost of living; however, you will find a financial necessity to cover your outreaches beginning day one. Never be afraid to ask for funds to accomplish God's work. This was a difficult lesson for Pastor M and me to learn. We have always been self-sufficient, and if we needed extra funds, I simply added a part-time job to earn what we needed. This mentality was very hard to overcome, and God needed to deal with it.

The most important thing to remember is that when we do not ask for help, we are denying people their blessings of both generosity and participation in God's plan. Whenever we really needed something, God provided it—not once in a while but every single time, and usually through someone we had never met. We as Christians are all part of God's family and His team. We should therefore all be of one heart and mind when it comes to bringing a dying world to know Him and His love, mercy, and forgiveness.

You must also be equipped and ready to bridge the culture gap as a foreigner. One of the best ways to begin this process is to throw a Matthew Party. I previously mentioned that we used this technique in Haiti with marginal success. Different parts of the world will respond differently to the idea, but it is certainly worth a try. Remember, when Jesus called Matthew to be His disciple, he was a tax collector, a job for which he was hated by the Jews. He was viewed as a pariah, a complicit collaborator with the Roman occupiers. That evening Jesus ate at Matthew's home with many sinners. When He heard the derogatory remarks from the Pharisees, He replied, "It is not the healthy who need a doctor, but the sick. But go and learn what this means: 'I desire mercy, not sacrifice.' For I have not come to call the righteous, but sinners" (Matthew 9:12–13).

This is a great way to break the ice with your neighbors. Throw a party with a lot of food, and invite everyone, not just members of the church. You may also want to consider teaching English to both children and adults in separate settings. This is a wonderful way to gain respect and authority while creating lasting friendships. If food is in short supply, consider a feeding program for the children as well. Jesus always met people's needs before He instructed them. This most certainly is a partial list; please feel free to ask for further guidance.

In His love,
Pastor D

My Dearest Macy and Mark

Well, here we are, three years later at the end of your instruction. I cannot express how incredibly proud we are of you. I have such peace concerning your mission, and I know that you are prepared. I cannot adequately express the overflowing joy my heart experienced when you shared about your upcoming nuptials. Yes, of course we will fly out for your graduation and wedding. We are excited to see you both and look forward to meeting your friends and family.

One of my last pieces of advice is to pray for God to give you your proclamation. A proclamation is a powerful word from God concerning your immediate future—in your case, your transition into your first mission post. The following was our proclamation as we entered Haiti into full-time ministry.

Lesson 30: Proclaim What the Lord Has Done

Retaking Eden—We Are Coming!

> We will give you every place where you set your foot. (Joshua 1:3)

When last we met, you left me broken and bloodied. You kicked me; you spat on me and called me names. You left me in a paralysis of cathartic sorrow and anguish so intense that I ceaselessly wailed, crying out for mercy and longing for a quick end. You thought to destroy us all, one by one; we are coming.

You may laugh the liar's scornful laugh because you think your victory complete; yet you forget to whom we belong: princes and princesses one and all; children of the one true King. You cannot have my wife, my children, or their families. You cannot have those we love or our disciples, our leaders, our missionaries, our staff, our brothers and sisters in Christ; we are coming.

You see that there is something much different now. You thought to destroy us, but our Father made us stronger. You see, we now fight with two things we sorely lacked last time we met: patience and humility. The armor is being polished, the shield shined, and the sword sharpened in preparation for battle, but this time it is not we who will wield the sword. We stand with our feet planted firmly on the Rock, patiently awaiting the call. We will not ride, we will not act, until we see the Lion of Judah leading the charge; we are coming.

You see, you angered our heavenly Father, and we have a good, good Father! We are coming to share His Fruit. We are coming to love the untouchables, the unloved, the lost, the unwanted, the forgotten, the sick, the diseased, the hurting, the slaves, the prisoners, the widows, the orphans, and the unsaved. We are coming with His power and anointing, equipped in the fivefold ministry, no longer fearful of His gifts because all our trust is now in Him. We are coming for His children, and we will not be alone! Already, I can feel the soldiers awakening as the Holy Spirit tugs at their hearts. We are coming to retake Eden and usher in His kingdom. You must just accept that you simply failed. You see, we are coming, and we all know how your story ends!

———— ◆◆◆◆ ————

This proclamation was true for Haiti and is still true as we prepare for God to open up Uganda and wherever else He would have us serve. It is the answer stated in Isaiah 6:8: "Then I heard the voice of the Lord saying, 'Whom shall I send? And who will go for us?' and I said, 'Here am I. Send me!'"

Enjoy this time serving the Lord. It is the most special time of your life, and it will pass all too quickly. I have focused on the many challenges you may face; however, your primary job is to spread the good news of the gospel of Jesus Christ. This is my commission to you here at the end of our training: Make as many disciples as you are able, and love all those God gives you. Live each day in purity of heart and with the utmost confidence that God has you. Laugh and play as often as you can. Speak boldly, with the authority given to you by the Lord himself. You are now commissioned officers in God's army and carry great responsibility. Your reward awaits you in heaven, but also in your post, as you will live how God intended. We are only a message away, and we will faithfully be covering you in daily prayer.

We love you both so much, and we will see you very soon.

In His love,

Pastor D

Epilogue

Saint Augustine once said, "A Christian is: a mind through which Christ thinks, a heart through which Christ loves, a voice through which Christ speaks, and a hand through which Christ helps." I wish this were true for all Christians, but it must be true for Christian missionaries. The advice I have given to Macy and Mark most certainly is not an all-inclusive list. There are so many events, mission teams, and children that it would be impossible for me to include them all.

There comes a time when children change; I call this time a "disconnect." In Haiti, the children most attached to us were tweens (ten to thirteen years old). In the United States, you could not have paid me enough money to teach this age group; however, in Haiti they were the sweetest and most lovable children. I only taught high school freshmen one very challenging year. Although I did not enjoy that year, God used it to bring forth Kefira, Sela, and Hannah.

The epitome of this age group in Haiti was Bonnie. Every other sentence uttered from her mouth seemed to be "Thank you, Pastor D" and "Thank you, Pastor M." She was present and active at almost every single event we held. Her greatest desire was to be able to give and receive love freely. At some time toward the end of a child's teen years the disconnect occurs, and his or her attitude typically changes to *What can you give me?* If we are not proactive, this same transformation occurs here in our children. The answer of course is more of Jesus, which is taught through relationship with our mentees and disciples.

Retaking Eden is a mindset, a total submission, which empowers our young to help usher in God's kingdom here on Earth. Our desire to retake Eden establishes vision and God-given assignments that line up with our creation purpose. Preparing and empowering our young adults may finally prepare the bride of Christ to receive her Groom. Blessings to you all!

About the Author

Pastor D is both a seasoned educator and hardened missionary warrior. He has spent the last ten years leading missionary teams into places most would not dare venture. His heart and desire are to help the next generation of missionaries prepare for what they will encounter, eventually passing the baton for their legs of God's great adventure in missions.

Printed in the United States
By Bookmasters